Donkeyness

Donkeyness

The Nature of Donkeys

Angela Dyer

Pelem Press

First published in 2012 by Pelem Press, London
pelempress@gmail.com

A catalogue record for this book is available from the British Library.

ISBN 978 0 9573748 0 5

Book designed by Robert Updegraff
Printed and bound in the UK by Biddles,
part of the MPG Books Group,
Bodmin and King's Lynn.

Frontispiece: Dulce

Contents

Introduction

There is nothing new about donkey worship; there's even a word for it, *onolatry*. Nor is there anything new about the abuse and ridicule handed out to these animals throughout history. Their relationship with man is longstanding and complex, as befits the donkey character – a character that is unique within the animal kingdom.

Much has already been written about donkeys. Anyone wanting to find out about particular breeds, their history or geographical distribution, or how to poultice a wound or pare a hoof, must look elsewhere. Indeed most donkey books tend to be strictly factual, when they are not sickly sentimental. Here I am attempting something different: to explore the nature of donkeys, their character, their unique essence, as well as examining their relationship with humans down the ages. Why do they hold the place they do in people's affections, while also being synonymous with stupidity and stubbornness? How is it that, patient and for the most part uncomplaining as donkeys are, they are so often the butt of extreme cruelty and neglect? Is any other animal so full of opposites, both in its own behaviour and in the way it is perceived?

In seeking answers to these questions I have drawn not only on my own first-hand knowledge of donkeys and on the experiences of other donkey owners, but more significantly on the place of these animals in art, legend and literature. It's a constant place but a modest one. The donkey is not usually foremost, is seldom in the limelight. It has to be sought out, wooed a little, encouraged. The carrot is more effective than the stick.

But first a few words about how the book came to be written. Like the path most favoured by donkeys, it was a zigzag one. The prime mover was my own donkey at the time, Dulce. Mooching restlessly one winter's day, wondering what to do next, I looked out of the window on my small farm in Andalucía and watched her as she grazed, so intent, so absorbed in what she was doing, had always done, would always do. I couldn't emulate this contentment – or containment perhaps, much more palpable than that of the other grazers – but could I capture it? Convey it?

The idea took root. In my naivety I saw this as *the* donkey book, until a preliminary trawl on the Internet brought me to my senses. At the touch of a button anyone could trace donkeys in Ireland and Iran, big donkeys and little donkeys, maltreated donkeys and pampered ones. So, laying aside the mountain of facts I had amassed (or rather, putting them on the compost to mature for a while), I decided to write from the heart, following my nose as Dulce followed hers.

This elegant donkey, introduced to a Cape winery to provide transport for wine-tasting treks, now follows in the footsteps of countless of its ancestors by helping to bring in the harvest.

The next setback was discovering that a book I would have been proud to have written was already in print. Someone lent me *The Wisdom of Donkeys* by Andy Merrifield, and after gobbling up the first few pages I was plunged into gloom. Here it was, a book about donkeys, recently and beautifully written, that not only conveyed much of what I already knew at first hand and had begun painstakingly to gather on the subject, but did so with originality and a depth that could not be matched.

Walking disconsolately up to Dulce's overnight field to fetch her for the daily graze, I stood at the gate and watched her make her most favoured descent in response to my call – not the obvious direct route to the gate but the higher one that meandered through three hairpin bends. Intent on her route, oblivious of time, undisturbed by her surroundings, she carried on. And as I watched her, the parable became clear and the gloom lifted.

By observing almost any animal on a daily basis one will learn things – about them and about oneself. With donkeys, aptly, the realisations come slowly. Time is unimportant. And yes, it is comforting to find that some of one's experiences are corroborated by the experts, and mildly irritating that other people have wandered down similar paths and found what one thought was one's very own. But if we take time to meander and browse, to pick other men's flowers as well as discovering some new ones, the rewards are high. For this donkey of mine was unique, our experiences together were unique, and between us we had something different to say. Our book would feature the donkey not, as so often, in a supporting role but centre stage, not as caricature or object of sentiment, not as butt for dubious humour or aid to self-enlightenment but as itself, in all its original, inimitable donkeyness.

Off for the day, Sathya Sai Sanctuary, Co. Sligo, Ireland.

CHAPTER 1

DONKEY
characteristics

That my donkey was unique became clear the more I read and heard about other donkeys. Making generalisations about them is as futile as making them about, say, the French. Apart from the basic facts of breed, physiology and background, every donkey is different. For as well as general characteristics, there is character to consider. And as with humans, character defines behaviour.

An Arab proverb says that the horse is God's gift to mankind, and biased though I am I have to admit that the ass often plays second fiddle to the horse, physically at least. It is as if God, when creating his bestiary, was wearied by the enormous effort he had put into designing that animal which could not be bettered, the horse, and he thought, Now, let's relax, have a bit of fun. Let this one have one outstanding feature, his ears; let him have a cry that will echo down the valleys and over the hills and always make man smile; let him be strong and for the most part willing; let him be hardy and sure-footed; but above all, let him have a character like no other animal.

There are, as we will see, many stereotypical characteristics attributed to donkeys – many of them negative – but among the positive ones what stands out most arrestingly is character itself. One might almost say *strength of* character, and it is this that accounts for much donkey behaviour often classed as negative. As a Jamaican proverb puts it, 'Every donkey hab 'im shankey' – knows its own mind.

No more than a few days old and raring to go.

Not surprisingly, a bad start in life will affect the disposition and temperament of the adult donkey – and here we are talking about domesticated donkeys, for wild ones have a different agenda. One that has been beaten, cowed, overworked or perhaps worst of all simply neglected, will almost certainly reflect this in its behaviour. It won't be a happy donkey, any more than a child similarly treated is likely to become a mellow adult. (There are no rules, and these of course are generalisations.) But what about the donkey that emerges from its exceptionally long stay in the womb, climbs on to its wobbly legs, gazes around – and almost immediately is looking for trouble? Admittedly this is more likely to be a male, ruled by testosterone almost from the start, it seems, and therefore less answerable for its social behaviour than its sister. Maybe the delinquent donkey's attitude is quickly picked up from the mother; not all female donkeys are natural mothers, any more than are their human counterparts. But I believe that there are cussed donkeys by nature just as there are cussed human beings, and that the best nurturing won't make much difference as to how they turn out in the long run.

Again, there are no rules. A Franciscan monk, Bartholomeus Anglicus, had a different view. Writing in the thirteenth century, he held that the donkey nature deteriorates with age. 'The ass is fair of shape and of disposition while he is young and tender, or [before] he pass into age. For the elder the ass is, the fouler he waxeth from day to day.' But his description of the treatment meted out to the poor animal, 'beaten with staves, sticked and pricked and led hither and thither', makes it all too understandable that he should end up 'a melancholy beast'. My own male donkey, who arrived aged one year as skinny as a toast-rack and seemingly devoid of testosterone, has since blossomed and become very full of himself. Though he is never likely to be beaten with staves, who knows whether in old age he will become as 'unlusty, dull and witless' as Bartholomeus's caricature.

The desire to caricature the donkey appears to be irresistible. In the West at least, its popular image is something of a dichotomy. On the one hand it is seen as sweet and innocent; on the other it is stubborn,

Neddie, an 'unwitting clown much loved for his eccentricities', was the most often adopted donkey at the Sathya Sai Sanctuary until his death in 2011 'at a great but unknown age'. No one knows how the ears came about.

wilful, or downright dangerous. In fact, donkeys – like all human beings worth knowing – are full of contradictions. 'Obstinacy with delicacy', says John Berger.

Delicacy, as she uses the very tip of a hind hoof to scratch so precisely that itch just above the left eyelid . . . 'I am such a tender ass, if my hair do but tickle me I must scratch', murmurs Bottom as he collapses into Titania's lap. Look at those slender legs, or listen to the tiny hoofs, shaped like a ballet dancer's block shoes, as the donkey trips lightly along a cobbled street – pitter-patter rather than clip-clop, hips swaying like a geisha girl in a too-tight kimono. And watch how this one extracts a chestnut from inside its nest of spines, or deftly gathers the few succulent stems of grass from within a patch of dross.

The donkey's obstinacy is legendary, and conjures up cartoon images of an animal with all four feet planted full square and a sweating red-faced yokel pulling fruitlessly at the reins. That it is fruitless is well documented. 'Cudgel thy brains no more about it, for your dull ass will not mend his pace with beating,' quips one of the clowns in *Hamlet*. 'If I had a donkey wot wouldn't go, D'ye think I'd wollop him? No, no, no . . .' went a surprisingly enlightened 1820s song. Robert Louis Stevenson, writing fifty years later, had more to learn when he bought a donkey to carry his baggage on a hike through the Cévennes in southern France. In a chapter headed 'The Green Donkey-Driver' he recounts his frustration at her chosen pace. 'What that pace was, there is no word mean enough to describe; it was something as much slower than a walk as a walk is slower than a run; it kept me hanging on each foot for an incredible length of time; in five minutes it exhausted the spirit and set up a fever in all the muscles of the leg.' The fact that the donkey, which he named Modestine, was 'not much bigger than a dog' and laden with 'a monstrous deck-cargo' does not seem to have given him pause for thought. On the advice of a passer-by he exchanges his cane for a switch, and in the next chapter, 'I Have a Goad', the switch for something more formidable. 'This plain wand, with an eighth of an inch of pin, was indeed a sceptre . . . Thenceforward Modestine was my slave.' Despite this bad start, Stevenson slowly learns how to adapt his own needs to those of his donkey – that is, to curb his impatience – and declares magnanimously at the end of his journey, 'Her faults were those of her race and sex; her virtues were her own.' He even sheds a self-conscious, if somewhat hypocritical, tear on leaving her. Donkey magic flowers in the most unpromising soil.

Modestine, engraving by Walter Crane as frontispiece to the 1907 edition of *Travels with a Donkey in the Cévennes* by R.L. Stevenson (see p. 100).

I too had to learn about donkey obstinacy the hard way – hard on the conscience, that is. On the few occasions when, as a novice, I lost my cool with Dulce – usually because of being short of time, a condition unknown to donkeys – it was I who ended up shaken and miserable; she just gave me a resigned look and carried on behaving exactly as she had been before the inexplicable outburst.

For what has so long been labelled obstinacy is, when looked at from the donkey's side of the fence, nothing more than an unbudgeable determination to stick to its own path. The donkey knows what is good, what is right, for him, now, at this moment – which may not be how it is in an hour's time, or tomorrow. If I have said that one of my reasons for keeping a donkey was to learn about myself, I must now confess that much of what I learnt was neither comfortable nor flattering. The desire to control, to be in charge, had to be slowly rooted out – simply because, in the face of a donkey's 'stubbornness', that is, its implacable knowledge of what it wants, control becomes an irrelevance. The most one can hope for in this animal relationship (as in its human counterpart?) is a mutual understanding where neither wins but both learn to give and take. In this way, I came to realise, both sides win.

Delicacy and obstinacy, yes; but also a great forbearance, a quiet, uncomplaining, almost dignified acceptance – of waiting, of rain or sun, of the folly and demands of human beings. This is another branch of what I have come to appreciate so much in donkeys, their 'dreaminess', a quality which Andy Merrifield likens to human reverie. The donkey will suddenly stop, to us inexplicably, and gaze off into far space, appearing to disappear. To me, this is the state induced by a truly good book: not a page-turner, but one that causes the reader frequently to pause, put the book down, look out of the window, ponder. Maybe for the donkey it is no more than Bottom's 'I have an exposition of sleep come upon me,' a sentiment shared by these patient animals down the ages, all over the world.

Allied to this is another quality typical of the donkey nature, imperturbability. Donkeys are not easily or quickly moved, physically or mentally. If faced with a new or puzzling situation they are more likely to stand and consider it than run away, as will a horse. They seem to be saying, it doesn't matter; not in our modern throw-away sense but rather, let it be, it will pass. This calmness of the donkey –

The epitome of containment, this little fellow photographed on a street in Fez remains unperturbed by his shackles and his burden.

which to its detractors may of course imply dullness – is reassuring and contagious, which is why donkeys are valued companions for the highly strung or distressed, both people and other animals.

But let's not get too carried away. There is, inevitably, another side. How about the perversity, malice even? My first exposure to the dual nature of the 'dear little donkey' came as a shock. In the field attached to a house we were renting in Spain was a particularly attractive Chagall-like donkey appropriately named Mon Cheri. We made acquaintance with him, and soon friends. Then one day he was not there. We searched among the herd of cattle with which he shared the field, but no donkey. So we went to the farmer to report his loss. 'Oh yes,' he said, 'Mon Cheri has had to go.' 'But why?' we asked. 'He killed two new-born calves.' 'But how?' 'Stamped them to death,' he replied. I think, then, I was a bit incredulous – but since having several times seen my own donkey (Dulce, meaning sweet and gentle) in full flight after a dog she had known for more than five years, at amazing speed and with deadly intent, I now know it was all too probable.

What motivates such behaviour, who knows. Do donkeys feel jealousy? Is it a sense of playfulness gone wild? A question of mood, or the phases of the moon? Certainly it is more likely to happen in a high wind, or when the donkey is disturbed for some reason – by the introduction of other animals or people, or change of any sort. Sometimes, and for no apparent reason, a madness seems to arise: the donkey will gallop at full speed, round and round if it is contained in a field, slithering to a halt inches from the fence before setting off on another circuit, head up, tail flying, braying and farting, possessed by some demonic presence. Then, as suddenly, the mood ceases, the head goes down, and peace is restored.

Signs of perversity occur on a daily basis – on good days it may be called a sense of humour, on bad ones something much darker is at work. And sometimes it is turned against the animal itself, as in the donkey which refuses to go inside the perfectly adequate shelter provided, preferring to spend the night with its back to a tree.

I spent a whole summer building a stable for Dulce. She loved it – the building of it, that is, appearing on site punctually every morning, inspecting new materials, nibbling bits of wood, once grabbing a cardboard box in her mouth and cavorting off in a flurry of nails. But when the shelter was made she never went inside it, whatever the weather, except to eat the bribes I put there in a futile attempt to get her accustomed to it. Someone suggested that perhaps the shed was too low, so when I moved I had another built, much higher. It turned out to be an expensive way of keeping her daily feed dry, for as soon as she had finished eating she would make off for her favoured tree, according to the direction of the wind. (And to prove the futility of generalising about donkey behaviour, my two French donkeys love their shelter, in fact hang around it a lot of the time like kids round the bike sheds at break, even – how shocked Dulce would be – piss in it at night.)

The melancholy associated with Eeyore is, like most characteristics attributed to donkeys, only half the picture. Yes, there is a sadness about the eyes, a 'sadness glowing at the far end of the long look that goes back to their remote beginning', and sometimes in the resigned droop of the stance. Patience and forbearance are passive qualities after all – and donkeys in all parts of the world, abused and mistreated, have reason to be sad. But the joker is there, waiting its turn and never absent for long, to make an appearance with a grab at the paper bag, a dive through the gate, a nip on the elbow: donkey keepers all have a list of their own. As Henri Bosco tells it, waiting 'to pass a muddy pond and go wallowing in it with their whole load on their backs.'

Joker is not the word used by my horse-loving friend as she gives 'one of many' examples of donkey behaviour. One day, riding a skittish young horse down one of the narrow walled tracks that crisscross that part of Andalucía, she saw what appeared to be a large sheet of corrugated iron on legs coming towards her. The man leading the apparition realised that it was likely to cause a problem, so he pulled on to a convenient verge and waited for her to pass. The iron, bent longitudinally and tied round the middle, was so long that neither end of the donkey bearing it was visible. The horse, deciding that a still sheet of corrugated iron was not so very alarming, was preparing to sidle by and had got exactly half way, too far on to go back but not yet past, when the donkey gave an enormous shudder. . . . The rest doesn't need telling.

Stories like this may sound to the uninitiated like one-offs, coincidences, but they occur too regularly, too often to be discounted as such. My favourite contribution from Dulce came the day after I had decided that she was getting fat and had contained her, so I thought, in a field with very little grass. A strange noise alerted me to the fact that not only had she got out, but she had removed the lid from a metal bin and was happily up to her neck in chicken feed. And for anyone who doubts the gremlin in the donkey make-up, the exact same thing happened again several weeks later, *as I was typing those very words*.

◆ ◆ ◆

Despite the 'stupid ass' label, donkeys are often attributed with high levels of intelligence by their keepers. From the Biblical legends of Balaam, and the braying ass alerting the sleeping Holy Family, stories of donkeys saving their owners, or attracting their attention in dangerous situations, are legion.

This miniature from a fourteenth-century Spanish Bible is entitled *Balaam and the Angel* but it is clearly the donkey that is at the centre of the drama.

Sue Paling, who runs with the help of volunteers a small sanctuary in Co. Sligo, Ireland, tells of a young donkey, Benny, who had befriended a much older horse, the mare Tessa. Alerted by 'a very agitated Benny banging on the metal gate with his hoof and snorting and braying', Sue followed him up the hill to where she found Tessa lying on one side with a badly bleeding leg. Leaving Benny 'standing over Tessa, nuzzling her neck and making sure none of the other, now curious, donkeys came too near', Sue went to get her first-aid kit. Having assessed the damage and bandaged the leg she decided that she could walk the mare down to the stables if she could once get her on her feet. 'Despite all my efforts she was not budging – until Benny took over. He literally shoved at her with his muzzle, nipped her neck and rump and generally annoyed her to the extent she heaved herself to her feet and began a slow descent, with Benny pushing and nipping constantly from behind.' For the next few days he visited her regularly, but as Tessa recovered he came less frequently, ultimately joining a band of young donkeys and going his own way.

Nurturing comes naturally to donkeys. Besides acting as guards for flocks of sheep or goats, they will often take on orphans, and not only of their own kind. A friend tells of an orphaned fawn coming in from the wild to sleep every night with a female donkey, seeking her out if she had moved field – and disappearing in the morning as soon as the farm came alive.

Intelligence is a dodgy word to apply to animals. Much animal behaviour labelled intelligent is more to do with their ability to adapt to the needs and desires of their owners. Is the poodle begging for a treat or the seal jumping through a hoop more 'intelligent' than a salmon returning 3,000 miles to its exact place of spawning four years previously, or a swift crossing continents to refind its nest year after year? That a donkey's manifestation of intelligence is often not in line with what its handler desires, does not justify labelling it stupid. Rather the reverse, one might claim.

Those who doubt the donkey's intelligence should watch one undoing a gate – preferably a gate that has been tied up by someone who knows about the Houdini-like capabilities of the donkey and who believes it has been made secure. I once watched powerless as Dulce, having unknown to me negotiated two of these, gave a nudge to the final one that had been left on the latch and disappeared off down the road with that typically derisive sideways flourish of the hind legs. Silly ass?

My own view of the donkey nature has inevitably been coloured by my first-hand experience of those I have cared for. As Dulce and her two offspring, male and female, were a particularly feisty trio, I became attuned more to the 'difficult' than the 'easy' label. This is not necessarily a negative: as with humans, the more difficult they are the more interesting they are likely to be. After all, wouldn't Eeyore's weary compliance become deeply irritating in the long term? Yet the two French donkeys I now look after – one can never claim to 'own' a donkey – are neither weary nor compliant, but are more polite than Dulce was. Perhaps it's a matter of imbibing the culture.

The wide-eyed innocence of the young donkey, most often associated with pampered Western pets, is just as evident in this woolly páramo that lives at altitudes of up to 3,000 metres in the alpine tundra of South and Central America.

One of the received wisdoms about donkeys is that they will pine unless they are with others of their kind. Yes, they do need and openly appreciate company, but Dulce was crotchety with both her foals right from the start. 'Me first' was the maternal rule, and this became acute and at times aggressive as the foals got older and more independent. After weaning she mourned for a day or two, and then appeared to settle happily back into her old routine where she was the sole boss, sharing her life only with me, the dogs and some sheep. She would bray twice a day, regular as an alarm clock, for food and attention, have an attack of the mads when the wind got up, enjoyed a walk with the dogs when one was on offer, and a day out at a feria even more. She carried her own water up to the night field, though this was the only work she did – and surely it was only the tattered remains of my own Protestant work ethic that suggested she would be happier if she worked more. All in all she appeared to be a thoroughly contented donkey. Maybe she, like her owner, enjoyed company but found it taxing to live with anyone of her own kind.

Another characteristic often attributed to donkeys is innocence. Why innocence? How can innocence be combined with such knowingness? Yet I think few would argue that the donkey appears 'innocent' in a way that a horse, for instance, does not, nor a cow, nor a dog. Maybe it is to do with physiognomy – those wide eyes, the air of vulnerability.

We are accustomed to seeing the donkey portrayed with head bowed, submissive, lowly, whether bearing the pregnant Virgin or a pile of garbage. Perhaps it is this submissiveness that suggests the dignity associated with donkeys. For these animals share with the oppressed and ill-used, human and animal, over the centuries, a resigned stoop that nevertheless conveys great dignity. Or should we call it gravity? It's an enclosed quality, born of the need to withdraw from the cruelty of the world into an inner, private place. In whatever situation devised by man the donkey finds itself – and these vary from the merely degrading to the utterly horrific – it manages to maintain its self-composure. It is as if the indignities wash round it, leaving it untouched. Modestine, Balthazar, the unnnamed donkey in the brick kiln or on the beach, even Eeyore with a bow on his tail, all succeed in preserving this core quality, whatever we choose to label it.

CHAPTER 2

DONKEY
physique

Donkeys are very four-square. They do quite often roll – a sensual exercise, with much voluptuous groaning – and in order to regain their feet may sit up for a few moments in a caricateurish sort of way, but for the most part they are solidly earthbound. ('Keep all four feet firmly on the ground' is the advice of the fabled Blue Donkey to the seekers after truth.) Except when very young they do not prance but prefer to amble – to plod, some would say – and the head is typically held low, in keeping with their characteristic humility. They are less flighty, physically and mentally, than their equine cousins. 'Horses are for hurrying ahead of the others', says the Sufi mystic Rumi. To which one might reply, 'Donkeys are for wandering alongside.'

This sturdiness has much to do with their body shape, which is less curvaceous than horses'. Donkeys have hardly any withers, and the whole back is flatter than that of a horse. Indeed, many appear almost two-dimensional, tough creatures not much more than bone and muscle, though others, overfed and underused, may develop rolls of fat along the neck and on the rump.

One of the donkey's chief attributes is its hardiness and agility over rough terrain. Crucial to this are the legs. Whatever the animal's size, a donkey's legs are a masterpiece of engineering. They are understated: shorter and stockier in relation to the body than those of a horse, they are physiologically similar but designed to carry more weight and to make the donkey more agile – 'legs for crossing mountains no horse could tackle', as John Berger puts it. Though some of the large breeds, the French Poitou in particular, may be 'hairy about the hocks' – a euphemism for lack of breeding applied to women in Victorian England – most donkeys' legs are neat and businesslike, as are their hoofs unless neglected.

The donkey's agility and sangfroid is typified in this painting by Horace Moore-Jones of a wounded soldier being carried to safety above Anzac Cove (see p.73).

Many of the donkeys taken into sanctuaries – and many more, less fortunate – have hoof problems. This is partly due to their being kept in conditions alien to their native habitat where the climate is hot and dry and the ground correspondingly hard. When they live on wet land their hoofs lack the natural daily abrasion that is necessary to keep them in good health and shape, and in places such as Ireland – where donkeys have been recorded since the Middle Ages – the soil is likely also to be acid, which adds further complications. Over time, if they are not cared for and regularly trimmed, the hoofs become hideously overgrown and malformed, the bones inside often being irreparably damaged and causing the animal untold pain. Sue Paling records a donkey with hoofs an unimaginable 40.5cm long. The hoofs of a well-tended donkey are particularly appealing in their neat compactness, which makes such a grotesquely deformed state an even greater obscenity.

Large working donkeys such as this were highly prized – and priced: in France a Poitou 'jack', kept to sire mules, was worth a staggering 2,400 francs at a time when a working horse fetched 150 francs and an ox 160 francs. In 1906 a Poitou was sold to an American buyer for 10,000 francs, only to die on board ship on its way to the US.

But however much we admire the donkey's sturdy body, it is the head that is its most appealing feature, for here we see the character. And, as with humans, the character, the essence, is in the eyes. A donkey's eyes are very deep – unfathomable, in fact, but inviting such poetic similes. 'Like two black-crystal scarabs' says Juan Ramón Jiménez of Platero's eyes, while Balo's in *The Donkey Who Always Complained* are likened to black wells under the moon. 'Like two dark truffles buried deep in a hairy undergrowth', writes Andy Merrifield – but the eyes of the huge-headed, smooth-haired Andalusian donkey, not buried at all, are just as profound. These donkey eyes are extraordinarily expressive, much more so than the eyes of a horse or a cow: they can convey resignation, fear, mischief, trust. The muzzle, similar to that of a horse, demands to be felt – and indeed resembles felt – so soft that it feels almost damp, as a dog's belly does. And then, those ears!

'. . . and kiss thy fair large ears, my gentle joy,' croons Titania over Bottom's ass's head. But why the size? For most of Nature's wilder excesses there is a purpose, a reason: the giraffe's neck, the elephant's trunk, the pelican's beak, three that spring to mind of surely thousands that are instrumental to an animal's survival. But a donkey's ears? Yes, donkeys in the wild need to be able to hear well in order to locate possible predators; but so do many other animals with modest ears, and for the donkey the senses of sight and smell are just as important. The ears, like those of another large-eared animal, the elephant, do play a part in cooling the blood, which obviously served a purpose for donkeys in their native habitats. Whatever their use, or lack of it, the disproportionate ears – even more obvious on a foal – are the hallmark, the signature, of the donkey. By your ears are you known.

(I recall the visceral punch of a photograph used to raise funds for an anti-cruelty campaign, showing a donkey with its ears sawn off – the mind catching up slowly, wondering what this could mean not only for the donkey but for the soul of the perpetrator. For most donkeys do not like their ears being touched at all, however gently – or even kissed, Titania – though they enjoy a scratch at the base of them or the poll in between.)

The Poitou is distinguished by its size, sturdy legs and long, matted coat.

Physiologically the donkey is more similar to the zebra than the horse. This is particularly true of both mane and tail. The mane is stubby and upright, with none of the flowing locks that adorn its more glamorous fellow equines, nor even a true forelock. What the donkey often does have though is a furry forehead; in fact it is more of a topknot, and in most foals as well as some adults the whole top part of the head is covered with dense hair, giving an irresistibly endearing look – a misleading butter-wouldn't-melt-in-the-mouth quality.

The tail, long-haired for only about half of its length, is a ferocious fly-swatter, with a side to side windscreen-wiper action across the flanks occasionally interspersed by a rapid and deadly accurate swipe between the legs. Any fly successfully dodging this may be reached by a lightning-fast flash of the teeth, which manage to reach to most parts of the donkey's lower body. But the flies always escape, and in the heat of summer when they are particularly troublesome the donkey will either choose a sandy patch or dig one up with its hoofs, sink into it, and swish the dust up round its body with the tail. Sometimes, when all this fails and the flies are winning by their sheer numbers, the donkey will become so enraged that it takes off, tail in the air, in a flurry of bucking and kicking that brings relief for a few moments.

Donkeys carry their foals for over a year, often as long as thirteen months, and the young are born perfect, new-minted, every hair shining – and raring to go. The head, ears and legs are particularly large at birth, and it can take up to six months for the body to catch up. The young will suckle for as long as their mothers will allow, often for six months or more. Donkey milk is particularly rich in albumin and contains more sugar and protein than cows' milk. This not only gives the young donkeys a good start in life but is a bonus for humans with special dietary needs, such as infants with food allergies; it is also used in the treatment of bone conditions and premature senescence. Donkey milk fetches extraordinary prices: milk from a small Balkan herd, kept specially for the purpose, cost €40 per litre in 2010, and a cheese made from it was claimed to be the most expensive in the world at €1,000 a kilo. The milk has long been enjoyed for bathing in by the rich and famous (p.75), and is still used by the cosmetics industry in France and Italy. Sperm from the Tibetan donkey was also considered to be of value for whitening the skin, when such a thing was fashionable.

Nowadays there are, in Europe at least, restrictions on the weight a donkey may be asked to carry. Obviously this must depend on the size and strength of the animal, and no one would defend a 10-stone man riding a Sicilian miniature – though many have, and still do. But given the size of an Andalusian Giant, for example, it is surely absurd to say that no one over the weight of 8½ stone (55 kilos) may ride a donkey. Historically, this would not only have ruled out Jesus, but probably also the heavily pregnant Mary, and their donkeys were not of the mammoth variety. A painting of Lord Burghley in mid-sixteenth century shows him, plumped up with finery and self-importance, swamping the little animal he is riding, though the 'donkey' looks more like a pony with donkey's ears than the real thing. (The caption to the picture reads 'No donkey', but in the context I think this applies to Burghley rather than to his mount.)

So donkeys down the ages continue to carry their loads, both physical and metaphorical, stoically and for the most part without complaining, knowing – as others have more laboriously to learn – that complaint often only leads to further misuse.

CHAPTER 3

DONKEY
habits

Donkeys are tidy in their habits. Unlike horses, which scatter their droppings anywhere and everywhere – particularly happily it seems on formal, ceremonial occasions – donkeys prefer to leave their neatly formed, shiny faeces, roughly the shape and size of anthracite, in a certain place and will often hang on for a long time in order to do so. The young learn to do this from a very early age, dropping their broad-bean-sized offerings alongside those of their mother. As well as avoiding the whole pasture being fouled this is handy for manure collection, though because donkeys' digestion is so thorough, there is much less goodness left in their manure than in that of horses.

Although the donkey's ability to survive on very little food is undisputed – the quality that has made it so valued as a work animal on poor land – equally undisputed among donkey owners is their interest in food. (The war baby can never get enough chocolate?) This can be a useful tool, but feeding a donkey titbits casually can turn it into a menace, and it will not be subtle in its demands. One of the donkeys taken in by Elisabeth Svendsen, founder of the first donkey sanctuary in the UK, had been owned by a publican, who warned her that it would need its daily pint of beer. Sure enough, on arrival the donkey became so vociferous and aggressive in its demands that they were forced to give him his pint to calm him down – a habit that took three months to break. Nor was this a unique case; the sanctuary has since had a further two alcoholic donkeys, and a rather obviously posed photograph taken around 1900 in the US shows a donkey tucking into a bottle of beer.

The muzzle and mouth of a donkey are particularly appealing. Those lips, so velvet soft, so sensitive as she eats a plum then delicately spits out the stone. How then the prickles? Gorse, thistles (the small yellow ones prevalent in Spain in late summer cannot be touched without wearing gloves) and sarsaparilla, a climbing plant with innocent heart-shaped leaves on a stalk of diabolical spines that will pierce a leather glove and easily take out an eye – all are grist to the donkey mill. True, they demand special treatment: head raised, lips splayed, teeth bared a little and a look of steady concentration, all reminiscent of Grandma extracting a raspberry pip from under her dentures; but down they go, slowly and carefully, barbs and all.

Watching a donkey forage and graze is a relaxing pastime, almost a meditation – and, like meditation, never to be undertaken if one is in a hurry. Here eyes and nose work in tandem: that lush-looking plant that she sees out of the corner of her eye and pulls towards will be instantly passed over if it does not smell good. And it is here, when grazing – especially in long grass or hedgerows – that the donkey's delicacy is paramount. The ability to use nose, lips, mouth and teeth, clumsy instruments at first sight, to extract with absolute precision the luscious morsel from inside a dense clump of undesirable growth never fails to impress me. Guided by the nose, the lips curl and grasp the chosen stalks, the mouth jerks them away from the rest, perfectly judging the firmness or delicacy needed to do so – and if occasionally a piece of earthy root clings to the end of the grass, this is smartly ejected out of one side of the mouth with a deadly chomp of the guillotine molars. Very short grass calls for a different technique, more like that of sheep or goats, with just the front teeth nibbling the turf. And this motion is further refined when in the height of summer there seems to be little but dust on the ground, yet somehow the donkey manages to use lips and front teeth to suck up and filter any seeds that are still available.

This is why artificial feeding can never replace natural grazing. The instinctive search for the best nourishment available according to site

and season is the most basic, and therefore one must presume the most satisfying, drive known to grazing animals. It is what they do, almost what they are. And like most grazing animals donkeys will not, unless desperately short of food, crop to the bone since they 'know' that the next meal depends upon the grass continuing to grow.

Donkeys have an acute sense of smell. Besides being a guide to what is edible and what should be avoided – and what is lurking in the pocket of any bystander – the nose is used in greeting and assessing other equines, who both smell and blow into each other's noses. It is also employed in a Hoover-like action along the ground to detect the passing of other animals, a useful tool for donkeys in the wild. Whenever we went on a track where other donkeys, mules or horses had passed, I got used to allowing Dulce to take her time sniffing their droppings, having learnt that any effort to hurry along this process would only end in a fruitless tussle.

The donkey's reputation for melancholy, justified or not, must be partly attributable to its bray. This extraordinary noise, with its long wind-up and blistering crescendo, often dying

Perhaps the earliest of many blue donkeys is this onager, seen in full bray on a medieval manuscript.

away in something like a death agony, is distinctive and unique. We are told that the bray can be heard up to three kilometres away, a useful tool when the wild animals, which tended to live more spread out than horses, wanted to make contact. (A legend had it that the onager, a wild ass, brayed twelve times to mark the hours leading up to the spring equinox.) The much parodied 'hee-haw' comes about because the noise, unusually, is made on both ingoing and outgoing breaths. To call a donkey's bray an 'eeyore' is to reduce and infantilise

it. 'A voice like a ferry departing', writes Sue Paling, more accurately and robustly, or a rusty pump-house engine according to Ted Hughes.

Donkeys live for donkeys' years. Thirty to forty years is the norm if they are well looked after, and some live much longer, even into the sixties. The current world record is claimed by a donkey in Colorado called Flower, whose birth date is recorded as 1941 and who is thought to be a descendant of the donkeys used in the Colorado gold rush (p.57). In keeping with their longevity, and like elephants, donkeys have impressive memories: they have been proven to be able to remember – that is, recognise – places, people and other donkeys after twenty-five years or more. This seems to me to be in keeping with their 'old soul', both individually and as a race: they have been around for a long time; they carry a lot with them.

CHAPTER 4

DONKEY
names

The word donkey is relatively new – it came into use in the late eighteenth century, when it was pronounced to rhyme with monkey. Until then, in legend, in the Bible, in Shakespeare, the donkey was an ass. One can't help wondering, given the pejorative use now of that word both as idiot and as corruption of arse, whether the donkey would hold the place it does in modern affections, anyway in the Western world, if it had remained an ass. In fact one could claim that the ass/donkey nomenclature defines the difference between the stupid ass of the past – beast of burden, object of ridicule – and the 'dear little donkey' of current myth. It is hard to imagine an Ass Sanctuary getting to the hearts and pockets of as many people as the donkey sanctuaries succeed in doing.

Where 'donkey' came from is more difficult to discover – surprisingly so, given its recent appearance. The Oxford English Dictionary associates it, with its monkey pronunciation, with the proper name Duncan, but gives no reason for this. (Though the coat of arms of a branch of the clan Duncan from the Hebridean island of Iona, with variations on the name which include Donkey, Donken and Downkin, has as its motto *Disce pati*, Learn to suffer, which fits the donkey nature very neatly.)

A more likely derivation is from the Celtic *dun*, meaning small brown, and *quai*, small – a double diminutive which also seems to suit the donkey. Another source could be the Flemish word *donnekijn*. In Scotland the donkey is known as a cuddie, and the word moke,

The dilemma faced by Buridan's ass provides visual scope for the cartoonist, here parodying the decision facing the US Senate as to the best route for a proposed new canal, see p.106.

generally associated with gypsies, is a derivation of the Welsh word for ass, *mokhio*. The Spanish word, burro, is in such common use throughout the world that it no longer needs italics. *A Classical Dictionary of the Vulgar Tongue*, published in 1785, suggests that donkey might derive from the Spanish *don*, 'for the don-like gravity of that animal', adding that it was also known as the king of Spain's trumpeter. As for the word ass, Isidor of Seville, writing in the seventh century, says that it came from *asedus*, from *sedendo* meaning sitting, clearly a dig at the donkey's reluctance to move under command.

Pet names for donkeys include Neddy and Dicky, both males – which brings us to Jack, short for jackass, the male donkey, 'jack' being used in the names of various animals, birds and fishes to signify either maleness or smallness. Many fictional names seem equally obscure, though a few stand out, see p.86

The use of the word ass, without apology or explanation needed, to signify a stupid person dates from the sixteenth century, and was freely used by Shakespeare in that sense. Still today the word ass is likely to be preceded by 'silly' or 'stupid', and donkey, though milder, has the same connotation. 'Asinine' is an adjective always used pejoratively. In the eponymous card game, the one who is out is the donkey. In poker, the unskilled player is a donkey. Donkey signifies dunce.

Which makes me wonder whether that word donkey, with its original pronunciation, might not have derived from 'dunce'. This word, which came from the Dunses, followers of the thirteenth-century Scottish theologian and philosopher John Duns Scotus, took on its current meaning of dullard or blockhead in the sixteenth century. A fine example of how words can come to stand for the opposite of their original meaning, since Duns Scotus was no slouch intellectually, and his nickname was Doctor Subtilis. (Duns Scotus was a contemporary of the French philosopher Jean Buridan, best known – despite a prodigious amount of other work – as the proposer of the paradox known as Buridan's ass: the donkey, placed at an equal distance between a pile of hay and a bucket of water, is unable to make the choice between the two, and so dies.)

But since donkeys usually have the final word, here is an anecdote recounted by Elisabeth Svendsen of the Devon Donkey Sanctuary. A man from Pontypool, weary of a lifetime of being labelled 'a donkey', decided that it was not to his family and friends that his money would go: he left everything he possessed to the sanctuary.

CHAPTER 5

DONKEY
work

The verbal associations with the much-maligned donkey, when not implying stupidity, are mostly to do with drudgery. The donkey engine, donkey pump, steam donkey, nodding donkey (a pumpjack), donkey stone (a scouring block), donkey jacket – all are sturdy, reliable but distinctly unglamorous, associated with hard work without much reward. Donkey work, in fact.

So before we consider the status of the donkey in a world in which, for the majority of people, it is an animal of the past, superseded by the tractor and the motorcar, let's take a brief look at its role as beast of burden since it was first domesticated so many thousands of years ago.

Exactly how many thousands seems to be a matter of huge discrepancy, with claims ranging from eight to nine – which takes us back to the very beginnings of agriculture – to a more probable six.

The earliest domesticated donkey bones so far identified date to between 4600 and 4000 BC, found at the site of El-Omari, a predynastic Maadi site in Upper Egypt near Cairo. The skeletons of ten donkeys were recently discovered in a burial complex of one of the first Egyptian pharaohs at Abydos, 500 kilometres south of Cairo. The tomb was probably that of King Narmer, founder of the first Dynasty who ruled around 3100 BC, or possibly of his son, King Hor-Aha. From the skeletons scientists were able to surmise that the donkeys would have been very similar to the Somali wild ass, still alive today, but the fact that the bones showed signs of considerable wear and tear (abrasion of the load-bearing joints, arthritis in the vertebrae behind the shoulders where a pack would have been placed), plus the fact that they were buried in such a sacred place, all indicate that these were domesticated, working donkeys and highly valued as such. 'It certainly suggests that they were of very great importance to the pharaoh and the early Egyptian state,' wrote Fiona Marshall, an anthropologist at Washington University, St Louis. '. . . having land-based transport of this kind helped to integrate the state, which was the world's first and earliest nation-state.'

A fourth Dynasty tomb (c.2500 BC) at Maidum, south of Cairo, has paintings of donkeys helping with the grain harvest, carrying sheaves and working on the threshing floor – some being as badly treated as at any time since, tugged and beaten for their pains. Rumi's rhetorical question, 'How just do you feel when you load a lame donkey?' is as pertinent today as it was more than three thousand years before he posed it.

Since the domestication of most species – cows, sheep, goats – took place from around 8000 BC in the Near East and in southwest Asia, it is surprising to find that the closest relatives to our domesticated donkeys today are the wild asses of northeastern Africa, the Nubian wild ass (*Equus africanus africanus*) and the Somalian (*E.a.somaliensis*). I think of these zebra-like animals as I brush my grey donkeys, the residual stripes on their legs and their white underbellies linking them over thousands of years and miles to their wild ancestors.

◆ ◆ ◆

A donkey is loaded with corn in this Egyptian wall painting from the 13th century BC.

· 37 ·

To Westerners today, donkeys have become almost synonymous with sanctuaries. For most of us, who eat too much, take too little exercise and suffer the consequent ailments, it is hard to imagine a life in which basic survival depends upon a donkey. Yet this is the case for countless people at the beginning of the twenty-first century. In many countries throughout the Middle East, Africa and Asia, owning a donkey can make the difference between eating and starving, life and death. And the fact that donkeys can be used for ploughing by women makes them more desirable than the alternative, oxen, which are both harder to handle and demand heavier equipment and harnesses. Donkeys are also more resistant to drought and disease than are oxen. According to an Ethiopian saying, 'An ox is for tomorrow but a donkey is for today.' In Niger and Burkina Faso, where traditional pits for making compost are once again being constructed, donkey carts play a role in transporting the manure that has to be spread in the bottom of the pits to attract termites.

In Nigeria donkeys are helping to solve a twenty-first century problem in a novel way: the Kano donkey is currently being used in an experimental programme for the collection and disposal of the vast amounts of household waste that are causing health problems in the area. (The expression 'He/she speaks Hausa like a Kano donkey' is not, as one might expect, similar to being called a fishwife but is in fact praise for foreigners fluent in the language.)

In Somalia, a project to supply donkeys to people in Dadaab Refugee Camp has been a lifeline. 'Since my group got a donkey and a cart, we are able to carry full rations of food home,' said a Somali woman refugee photographed standing proudly beside her new acquisitions. 'In addition, we are able to engage in small income-generating activities, such as carrying mud bricks for the construction of houses for a small fee, for people who are not part of our group.'

Another saying from Ethiopia, 'Donkeys do not have to eat honey', indicates that these animals are not pampered – and indeed, as the work of The Brooke and others makes clear, many of them are still shockingly badly treated. But as educational programmes increase and people realise that by caring for their working animals, whether donkeys, mules, horses or oxen, they will in fact get much more from them, one hopes that slowly their conditions will improve, even if only through the self-interest of their owners. To change a longstanding cultural attitude that gives the donkey no status except that of drudge will take longer.

The traditional role of the donkey as slave is alive, and only occasionally kicking, in many parts of the world. Susan Orlean gives a vivid description of her first encounter with what she came to realise was a commonplace in Fez. 'The donkey was small. His shoulders were about waist-high, no higher; his chest was narrow; his legs straight; his hooves quite delicate, about the size of a teacup. . . . The  televisions, however, were big – boxy tabletop sets, not portables. Four were loaded on the donkey's back, secured in a crazy jumble by a tangle of plastic twine and bungee cords. The remaining two were attached to the donkey's flanks, one on each side, like panniers on a bicycle. The donkey stood squarely under this staggering load. He walked along steadily, making the turn crisply and then continuing up the smaller path, which was so steep that it had little stone stairs every yard or two where the gain was especially abrupt. I caught only a glimpse of his face as he passed, but it was utterly endearing, all at once serene and weary and determined.' An estimated 100,000 people in the Fez area rely for their livelihood on donkeys, which operate 'like little pistons, moving people and things to and fro'. Although poverty is what makes the donkey central to survival for so many people here in Morocco, it is not the only reason. As Orlean points out, 'The medina in Fez is now a World Heritage site. Its roads can never be widened, and they will never be changed; the donkeys might carry in computers and flat-screen televisions and satellite dishes and video equipment, but they will never be replaced.'

We have only considered Africa, and only a minute part of that huge continent. China is estimated to have over seven million donkeys, the majority of which are working animals, although the Chinese have another use for donkeys. Which brings us to a subject that is taboo in most of Europe as well as some parts of Africa and Asia. Donkey meat is rich in protein, usually tender (depending on the age and feeding of the animal), and of good flavour; to some, it stands up well to beef. So why the taboo?

A story from Zimbabwe underlines the prejudices associated with particular foods, and how these differ from culture to culture. In the current food crisis, craving food that he had been brought up on, a Zimbabwean man 'discovered cold meat that looked and tasted very much like what we used to call French Polony in Zimbabwe.' Waiting in the queue at his local butcher, he got into conversation with another man who asked what he intended to buy. 'I pointed to him the meat that had captured my heart. Nothing could have prepared me for what followed. In a very animated voice, the gentleman said, "O, yes, the Mortadella! That's very delicious! It's made from donkey meat, you know. It's a delicacy from Bologna . . . It is very good and healthy meat. In Italy they give it to children, because it's very good for the young ones. Good choice!" ' Our friend is stunned. 'I grew up with the knowledge that man does not eat donkey meat. If a donkey died it was simply buried. No one slaughtered a donkey for meat. With the image of the donkey firmly in my mind, I could hardly believe that I had actually consumed donkey meat. I shuddered at the thought. But the irony was that I had actually enjoyed it.'

In some, but not all parts of Namibia eating donkey meat is openly accepted; it is cooked like beef, with spices, and also dried to make a type of biltong. (The Namibian word for donkey meat is *him*, which might do more than anything else to put the English-speaking world off eating donkey meat.)

Most eating taboos are of religious origin. Muslims are presented with some contradictions on the subject of whether it is permissible to eat donkey meat, the safest path being to eat wild ass (onager) if you are inclined to, but avoid the meat of the domesticated donkey. In fact what happened is that when presented with wild donkey the Prophet declared it halaal, a ruling that has been maintained, whereas he later withdrew his permission to eat domesticated donkey meat. Jews too are forbidden to eat horse and donkey meat.

To most readers of this book the question will remain academic. But life in a harsh climate is itself harsh; droughts are frequent, crops fail, people go hungry – and hungry people will eat what they can. I would not like to pass judgement, for I could not say that if my children or grandchildren were wasting away from malnutrition I would deny them donkey meat. And that the thought is so horrifying to many who are happy to sit down to a Sunday roast of beef or mutton, itself says something about the Western relationship with the donkey – quite apart from the shrink-wrapped conception of food in general, when city children genuinely believe that milk arrives in cartons and eggs in boxes. For most of us fortunate ones a donkey is a friend, part of the family, and as such could not be eaten whatever the circumstances.

◆ ◆ ◆

I am often asked, 'What do you keep a donkey for?' Sometimes, more accusingly, 'What do you keep a donkey *for*?' An odd question, one never asked regarding dogs, or even horses. But because for so long donkeys have been very much *for* something, it is perhaps harder now to accept that they aren't, in the West, *for* anything – except, and always, for themselves. The answer I would give now would be in order to understand more, about donkeys and about myself: to recognise my impatience and need to control, neither of which cut any ice with the donkey's ancient wisdom, as well as more positive motives such as the desire to be close to an animal, to share experiences and to nurture.

As to why we keep pets, there is an instinct in most humans – particularly women and children – to befriend and care for animals. For adults they may be surrogate children, for the children themselves a lesson in caring. Whatever the motive, the concept of pets is relatively recent; the word itself, implying intimacy and indulgence, only came in at the beginning of the sixteenth century. This is not the impulse to study, collect, hunt or use animals, which is as old as history – and most often a male preserve – but rather to invite them to share one's life. In 2008 several English newspapers printed pictures of Holly and her colt, Charlie, who had the run of a

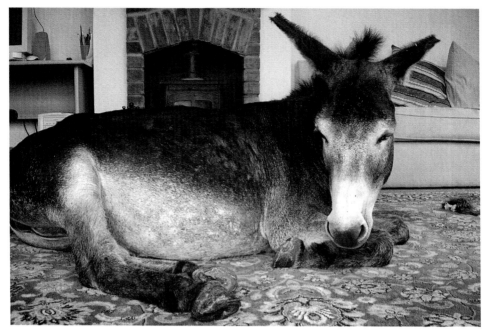

Holly makes herself at home.

household in Bude, Cornwall. Admittedly this was an unusual household that included sheep and assorted poultry along with two children and their dogs and cats, but it was only the donkeys that were invited to share family meals and watch television.

In the UK, an amazing three-quarters of the donkey population now grazes on land owned by the Donkey Sanctuary in Devon. The statistic makes the question 'What are donkeys for?' more pertinent. For what would one think of a country where three-quarters of the population lived in old people's homes? This is not strictly a fair parallel, as some of the inmates are healthy donkeys whose owners can no longer look after them, and one of the sanctuary's aims is to relocate them to homes where they will be well cared for, and even possibly worked. But there is something a little unsettling about the institutionalisation in such extreme numbers of an animal whose native habitat is untold hectares of open plain. True, the domestic donkey in the UK is unlikely to retain an imprint of this – and may indeed be fortunate to have seen any grass at all during its life – but there is about the sanctuary set-up, with its jolly newsletters and gift shops and knitted tea-cosy donkeys, something that to my mind is not quite in keeping with donkey dignity.

This small gripe aside, the Devon Sanctuary does an amazing job, and if some of the trappings of modern fundraising seem a little alien to the donkey's roots, neither the motivation nor the results can be questioned. And although Elisabeth Svendsen was the pioneer, her sanctuary is not by any means the only one. Throughout the UK you can find a host of small charities dedicated to the welfare of donkeys, run on a shoestring and supported solely by private donations. One such, the Michael Elliott Trust at Freshfields in Derbyshire, is run by John and Annie Stirling who spent their working life in the theatre and now rope in well-known actors to help raise money for their sanctuary. They report many donkeys currently being abandoned by people in financial trouble. 'There was one tied to our gate on Sunday morning, with a luggage note attached saying "Can't afford it".'

Sanctuaries have certainly caught the public imagination. They are astonishingly well supported, competing with and often outdoing many other good causes, as a correspondence in the *Guardian* made plain. A letter complaining that it was 'a national disgrace' that the British public gives more to donkey sanctuaries than it does to charities supporting female victims of abuse was met with a barrage of protest. One correspondent came up with a pragmatic solution. 'A small donkey sanctuary attached to say a refuge for abused women and children would have many benefits: the donkeys would be effective fundraisers, and helping to look after donkeys would be a positive and emotionally restoring activity for many abused adults and children.'

In places such as the UK where land is at a premium, lack of space necessitates rules and regulations – a situation that applies to the people of Britain as much as to its donkey population. In the US, where space is not an issue, many so-called sanctuaries are more like conservation areas, in which the animals are free to live almost wild. Some make lofty claims for mere donkeys. 'They came from a variety of backgrounds, in their own unique way, to be part of a mission of helping humans evolve,' declares one. Some confine their energies to neglected or abused domestic donkeys, others include in their programme the rescue and protection of wild burros.

The work of the indefatigable Elisabeth Svendsen has spread throughout Europe and as far afield as Kenya, Egypt, Mexico and India. In 2008 representatives of the Devon Sanctuary were invited to the first conference on donkey health and welfare ever to be held in China. Donkeys became a political issue in China in the year 2000, when a huge number of wild asses – an estimated 30,000 – poured over the Sino-Mongolian border into the Urad grasslands in search of food. Many returned when the grass gave out there too, but the Chinese, more kindly disposed towards donkeys than the Mongolians, provided an astonishing 130,000 hectares as a natural reserve for the animals.

(The Mongolians, 'a nation on horseback' who worship their horses, look down upon donkeys – in fact many regard them as scheming or even evil. A joke tells of a Mongolian who can't speak Chinese trying to communicate with a Chinese shopkeeper who speaks no Mongolian. Reduced to using sign language, the Mongolian points his second and third fingers at certain goods, to which the Chinese responds by showing his thumb and little finger. The Mongolian gesture refers to the Chinese as a sly donkey, while the Chinese is implying that the Mongolian is a stupid cow – insults that reflect the attitude of each nationality to these animals.)

Although it is sanctuaries that have captured the public imagination, lesser known organisations have been working for much longer to care for horses, mules and donkeys in places where they are vital to the economy.

In 1927 a wealthy American woman, Amy Bend Bishop, on a grand tour of Europe and the Mediterranean, was taken with the donkeys she saw in Fez. Disturbed by the condition of the animals – an estimated 40,000 donkeys and mules – she donated the equivalent of $100,000 to set up a free veterinary service in Fez. The American Fondouk (Arabic for inn) has been in operation ever since. Susan Orlean tells a delightful story of a donkey 'undergoing some sort of neurological crisis' arriving at the Fondouk under its own steam. Nor was it the only one; others may have been left at the gates by their owners in the early morning, but 'Fez and Morocco and the American Fondouk all seem to be magical places, and after spending even a few hours in Fez, the idea that animals find their own way to the Fondouk's shady courtyard doesn't seem unlikely at all.'

Similarly moved to put feelings into action was another indomitable woman, Dorothy Brooke, who in 1930 went to live in Cairo with her English cavalry-officer husband. A horse lover herself, she was shocked to find that hundreds, possibly thousands, of horses and donkeys, brought to Egypt during the First World War for use by the British, Australian and American armies, had been either sold into hard labour or abandoned. By 1934, her letters to the English press had raised enough money to open a veterinary hospital in Cairo. From there the work of The Brooke, with its headquarters in London now supported by fundraising branches in The Netherlands and the US, has spread through the Middle East southwards into Africa and east to India and Pakistan, with feelers also out in Latin America and further afield. In 2011 this highly professional charity was employing over a thousand staff, most of them locally based, focused on the welfare of working horses, donkeys and mules and on teaching their owners how to care for them, as well as lobbying institutions and governments and undertaking field research.

◆ ◆ ◆

Of the donkeys in the UK that remain privately owned, a surprising number do work for their living. On Blackheath in south-east London, donkey rides have been popular since the nineteenth century, when a gypsy family called the Boswells had a stand opposite the main gates of Greenwich Park. A typically slapstick description of a ride on the Heath by two Victorian ladies appears in Dickens's *Sketches by Boz*. The current Blackheath donkey man, Len Thorne, started working the donkeys when he was 14 and is still going strong at 78, despite a recent threat of his site being taken from him to make way for, ironically, an equestrian centre. 'I shall carry on until I drop down dead. It's my whole life. My best memories are seeing the delight of the children when they first have a ride, and knowing that my donkeys will always be a part of their childhood.' In London there are donkeys too at the City Farms that have in the past decades sprouted from the bricks and rubble as city dwellers labour to create oases of calm in a fast-moving world.

Although the rules and regulations that now strangulate a lot of mostly harmless fun have taken their toll on beach donkeys, you can still have a donkey ride on a few of England's beaches. (The longest living donkey in the UK is Lively Laddie, who worked on Blackpool beach until he was sent into retirement on the island of Sark, where he died aged 62. It can't have been such a bad life after all.) More acceptable now are beach walks – 'bring your own donkey or use ours' – organised by the Donkey Breed Society, which also runs a full programme of shows, meetings and events for donkey lovers in Britain. And if you live in the UK and want to organise a beach ride, fête or other social event, or an educational or advertising promotion featuring donkeys, or even make a film, all you have to do is contact Mike's Donkeys in Wales and as many immaculately groomed and apparelled donkeys as you wish will be delivered by horsebox – 'distance no problem'.

Ladies go sidesaddle on South Shields Sands, to the amusement of the onlookers (their maids, perhaps?). It was on this beach at the turn of the century that the young Jack Simpson worked as a donkey boy, see p.73.

One place where donkeys were used commercially until quite recently is Clovelly, in North Devon. This small and selfconsciously picturesque village built on a steep hill above the fishing port was restored in the mid-1880s, and though water and electricity were installed, the narrow cobbled streets have been retained. At that time donkeys were still used for transporting goods and people up to the village; for the downward route, it was sledges. Now, apart from the odd much-photographed donkey allowed to carry some light luggage up to the inn, most of Clovelly's working donkeys are no more than a tourist attraction, kept off the streets and used for carrying kids on prescribed rides and for pulling donkey carts.

High Street, Clovelly, c.1962.

Carisbrooke Castle, on a hilltop south of Newport on the Isle of Wight, still has its donkeys as it has for over five hundred years, though once again their function – of bringing up water by means of a tread-wheel – is now reduced to demonstrations and mere fodder for tourists' photos. A flourishing enterprise in Chalford, Gloucestershire, offers delivery of groceries and firewood by handsome donkeys wearing very fetching panniers. The days of the donkey as a working animal in the UK are not yet over, and indeed a new type of work has arisen.

Riding for the handicapped, on horses, has been successful for many years, but it took Elisabeth Svendsen to translate this to donkeys. As with her sanctuary she started off on a small scale, but the visits from a local school for children with both physical and mental learning difficulties were so successful that a charity was soon formed and – after a long battle with the planning authorities – a purpose-built centre was opened. Not content with providing mounts for those children capable of getting, and staying, on the donkeys, Mrs Svendsen commissioned a specially designed donkey trap that enables children in wheelchairs to get their thrill too. And thrill it is. Blind children, epileptics, those with cerebral palsy, autism, behavioural problems – all benefit from both riding and handling the donkeys, which is found to improve their balance, strength and co-ordination on a purely physical level, as well as increasing confidence and quietening anxiety. Not only have several more such centres been opened, but the Sanctuary staff also take the donkeys on visits to nursing homes, residential homes and hospices. Donkey therapy works.

◆ ◆ ◆

In other parts of Europe things remain more primitive in the donkey world. In Greece and Spain asses were traditionally used in vineyards, both for cultivating the vines and transporting the harvest, hence their association with Dionysos. They were also used – surprisingly, I thought, until I experienced at first hand their antipathy to dogs – as guards for cattle, sheep and goats against marauding dogs or wolves; certainly they would have been vociferous ones. In Andalucía donkeys are still used for transporting goods and people, mostly between villages and the plot of land that the older man of the family tends during the day. Being by nature convivial, few Spaniards choose to live in the country, preferring this arrangement which keeps the retired man out of his wife's way for most of the day while feeding the extended family, and enables them all to congregate in the bar or plaza at night. Now the donkey as the chosen means of transport for the smallholder has mostly been replaced by mopeds and quad bikes, but one can still see a donkey under a load of vegetables, fodder or firewood being led to the village, and often right through the house into a courtyard or stable behind. In my local town, the daily journey of one woman who still used her donkey for shopping was initially disrupted when a large roundabout was built, but soon afterwards the sight of dumps of manure around its verges showed that they had both learnt how to cope with this modern inconvenience.

Postcards from southern Spain show pannier-laden donkeys being used as specialist mobile shops up to the middle of the twentieth century: eggs, vegetables and coal in Córdoba, milk in Seville, pottery in Granada. Mijas, one of the White Towns inland from the Costa del Sol, is renowned for its numbered 'burro taxis' which carry visitors round the main square. The donkeys' ornate trappings ensure that their fame lives on, even if only as background colour in the inevitable tourist digital photo – and their welfare is now monitored by the local donkey sanctuary.

◆ ◆ ◆

Further afield, the role of the donkey is more down to earth. In many parts of Africa, in the Middle East, South America and in India donkeys remain vital to the economy, and to individual owners, as pack animals in the humdrum tasks of transporting food, water, firewood, and taking goods to and from market. They are used for carrying building materials, for drawing water from wells, and in India and Egypt for work in the brick kilns. But above all it is their agility on rough ground that has made them so indispensable to man.

So here, a small diversion to follow the donkey on its long journey from East Asia to Europe, along the Silk Road. By AD 200 a steady cavalcade of merchants and pack animals, bearing not only silk but spices, cloth, porcelain, paper, wine, musical instruments and much else, wound for 8,000 kilometres from East to West, linking the Imperial court of China to the Holy Roman Empire. From Byzantium, modern Istanbul, goods and animals spread further westwards through Greece, Italy, Spain and up through France to Britain. The route in fact resembled the silk that gave it its name: it began with hundreds of small strands or tracks from all over eastern China, was gathered into a thick skein in order to penetrate the formidable ranges of mountains that barred its way – the Pamir, Hindu Kush and Karakoram – from where it descended to the Indian subcontinent, loosening out once more into myriad tracks as it spread through Persia, Arabia and into Europe. One only has to imagine this journey to see what a crucial part the donkey must have played: bearing heavy – by modern standards, doubtless much too heavy – loads,

On the road to Kashgar, where donkeys are still a vital source of transport.

sure-footed on mountains and rough terrain, able to survive on sparse amounts of food and water, blessed with longevity. Perhaps after all it was not only God's sense of humour at work when he designed the donkey.

Though today the Silk Road is little more than a tourist attraction, donkeys still play an active part in the life of many of the places it passes through. Kashgar, at the crossroads of Central Asia, is famed for its Sunday bazaar which draws thousands of people, most of them in donkey carts. Donkey jams are frequent as the carts converge, overflowing with sprawling families bearing animals and goods to the market. Donkeys themselves are bought and sold in vast numbers each Sunday, and here one can buy the latest in (traditional) donkey harness and gear.

◆ ◆ ◆

Pictures of donkeys carrying large bundles of wood or piles of hay or tottering under loads of bricks proliferate, but they have carried some more unusual baggage. Remaining for a moment in Central Asia and in the twenty-first century, a cleaning-up exercise in the Karakoram mountains sponsored by National Geographic in 2012 used donkeys to help remove almost a tonne of garbage left by mountaineers and their entourages on K2; the spoil included car batteries, stoves, tins, bottles, fuel containers and plastic.

'The girl at the Bad Ass Coffee Co. tells me the donkeys were once used to haul coffee beans down the slopes of Mauna Kea', writes a contemporary poet about the donkeys of Hawaii; 'but now they are wild, and free to roam the lava fields, to graze on tufts of straw grass, the only thing that grows there.'

But let's go back to c.250 BC, and a papyrus written by a group of beekeepers in Philadelphia to a Greek official in Lower Egypt enquiring about the team of donkeys awaited to carry back their hives. The tone is urgent, since the peasants were threatening to 'release the water and burn the brushwood, so unless you remove [the hives] you will lose them.' Special carrying frames were constructed for the donkeys' backs, on to which the hives, probably made of pottery, were roped. Horses were occasionally used to carry hives too, but donkeys were favoured as being less liable to panic if things went wrong.

Donkeys have long been part of rural life in Ireland, where they were used to carry peat from the hills down to the villages and to haul coal from the mines. In England they transported manure to the fields, and another type of fertiliser, seaweed, from the beaches.

In the religious processions beloved by Catholics throughout the Mediterranean, donkeys bore the *cistae*, casks containing the sacred symbols, a solemn task which often gave way to snide jokes about priests and asses.

In rural France donkeys played a part in migrations both human and animal. In the eighteenth and nineteenth centuries migrant agricultural workers travelled huge distances looking for seasonal work on the land, using donkeys to carry their belongings as they journeyed from the plains where they had hoed, harvested and gleaned all summer, back to the wine-growing areas in time for the grape harvest. Another massive migration was, and still is, the movement of grazing animals from winter to summer pastures, and back again. In journeys that could last for weeks, huge herds of cattle, sheep and goats headed from all over the country for the lush pastures of the high Alps and the Pyrenees, where they spent the summer grazing. This transhumance took place as a natural migration long before it came to be orchestrated by humans, but once man became involved donkeys took their place, at the rear inevitably, as carriers of baggage and of the weak and sickly.

Donkeys contributed to 'one of the strangest sights on the main roads of France' when in the late eighteenth century the foundling hospital of Paris was forced by law to take in the flood of infants, orphaned or abandoned during this time of horrendous poverty, sweeping in from the provinces. 'Long-distance donkeys carrying panniers stuffed with babies came to the capital from as far away as Brittany, Lorraine and the Auvergne. The carters set out on their two-hundred-and-fifty-mile journeys with four or five babies to a basket, but in towns and villages along the route they struck deals with midwives and parents. For a small fee, they would push in a few extra babies. To make the load more tractable and easier on the ear, the babies were given wine instead of milk.' If this begins to sound like a Bacchanalian frolic, the reality was much grimmer. 'Those [babies] that died were dumped at the roadside like rotten apples. In Paris, the carters were paid by the head and evidently

Public shaming of debtors and other criminals, featuring gallows and pillories and with the culprits often mounted backwards on a donkey or a sow, were common in Europe from the mid-fourteenth century.

delivered enough to make it worth their while. But for every ten living babies that reached the capital, only one survived more than three days.' How the donkeys fared is not part of the story.

But perhaps an even stranger human cargo recorded in France a century earlier were the bankrupts who were mounted facing the donkey's tail and paraded throughout the town as a warning to all. In India even today, people are publicly shamed by being put on a donkey and led through the streets.

◆ ◆ ◆

Donkeys have always flourished in island communities, particularly small islands. They have a lot in common, besides their scale: separateness, containment, individuality. And because islands are inclined to be rugged they often present difficulties for motorised vehicles, agricultural and personal, giving an ideal opening for the donkey.

Animals bred over many years on small islands tend by selection, both natural due to the limited space and feed and man-made through preference, to become smaller themselves. In the Mediterranean, for instance, the donkeys on Sicily and Sardinia have become miniaturised to such an extent that an adult may be less than 80 centimetres at the withers. This makes them highly desirable as pets, and in 1929 a Sardinian miniature, one of six jennies and a jack to be imported to the US, gave birth to a foal – over four hundred years after the first donkeys, hefty animals from southern Spain, had been introduced by Christopher Columbus. Miniatures are now big business in America. The man who first imported them, Robert Green, was besotted, declaring that 'Miniature donkeys posses the affectionate nature of a Newfoundland [dog], the resignation of a cow, the durability of a mule, the courage of a tiger, and the intellectual capability only slightly inferior to man's.' Extravagant claims indeed.

Italian islands have produced four distinct breeds of donkey, from the dark, rangy animals of Pantelleria, to the Sicilian greys, to the elegant little Sardinians with their pastel colours and pronounced dorsal stripe, and the tiny pure white animals which give the island of Asinara its name. Spanish islands too have their distinctive breeds: the dark

Mallorcan donkey, up to a metre and a half high, and the much smaller Burro Majorero, indigenous to the Canary Islands and now in decline.

Although we must be pleased that people are cleaning up their act regarding donkey welfare, there is often a whiff of self-interest involved. A letter from the Central Government of Corfu to the Corfu Donkey Rescue, dated 28 July 2009 and available for all to see on the Internet, puts it bluntly: 'The Prefecture of Corfu appreciate the important work that you do – the looking after and saving of the donkeys which when they grow old are abandoned by their ungrateful owners – a work which contributes in the reduction of cases that would hurt the culture and the image of Corfu in the eyes of the tourists.' Well, maybe instead of getting high-minded about this we should see it as one of the positive results of tourism.

One Greek island where donkeys, along with mules, are still indispensable is Hydra. Here a forward-looking ecological programme has kept road building and motorised vehicles to the barest minimum (a few dust carts, the odd construction lorry and a fire engine), and all

This donkey appears to be completely at ease on the cliffs high above the Aegean on Amorgos, the easternmost island of the Cyclades.

other transport needs are fulfilled by mule and donkey. So donkey-orientated is the island that an international conference entitled 'The role of the donkey and the mule in the culture of the Mediterranean' was held there in 2009, with speakers from universities around the world delivering papers with suitably imposing academic titles. In more lyrical vein, Anne Michaels writes: 'On Idhra the pang of smells opened in me with the prickly sting of memory. Burros and dust, hot stones washed down with salt water.'

On the island of Santorini donkeys are a tourist attraction too, described as 'part of the island charm and loads of fun'. 'I thought it would be fun to hike up the steep path from the port to Santorini. Those donkeys are so cute,' warbles an enthusiastic tourist. The reality is a little different. For hundreds of years donkeys have been used to transport people and goods up the 680 cobbled steps from the harbour to the town of Fira. Who knows how they were treated in the days before tourism became the main source of income? Probably, knowing the attitude of the majority of Mediterranean people to animals in general and donkeys in particular, not well. Now things are improving for the donkeys, though slowly. A campaign run by the *Daily Express* newspaper in the UK brought the donkeys' plight to the public in 2007, with an article about a Greek vet who was attempting to educate the donkey owners as well as deal with some of the results of their neglect and cruelty. In 2008 a reporter who went back to see how things were progressing was threatened by an angry islander and told to go home. But by then the tireless team from the Donkey Sanctuary in Sidmouth had become involved, and the following year, besides setting up a programme of education and veterinary assistance, they contributed towards the cost of installing a cable car as an alternative means of transport up to Fira. Progress too is an uphill struggle, but it is being made.

On many more Greek islands – Crete, Spetses, Lesbos and others – donkeys are still a vital means of transport. On some, animals that were once turned loose and left to their own fate when they became too old for use are now sheltered and looked after, and the more able are given a new occupation as walking companions, carrying light loads such as picnics and tired children – a fine solution all round.

Donkeys have a long tradition of service in the Caribbean islands. Introduced by the Spanish around five hundred years ago, they were once an essential form of transport, but since this role was taken over by cars and buses they have been become redundant and mostly unwanted. Many were just turned loose to fend for themselves, others were sold for meat. In 2009 workers from Sidmouth set up a breeding programme in cooperation with the local government on Grand Turk, South Caicos and Salt Cay islands, thus saving these animals from almost certain slaughter. And the small island of Aruba has a sanctuary of its own, founded by two islanders who were distressed by seeing donkeys tied to trees and left to die.

Finally a story from the Galapagos Islands. In 1935 five young brothers from the Angermeyer family fled Nazi Germany and sailed to the islands in a boat bought by their parents with the proceeds of the family home. They settled and built a house on Santa Cruz. Whenever they needed help with transport or haulage, they simply caught one or more of the semi-wild donkeys on the island, turning them loose again when the task was completed.

◆ ◆ ◆

This habit of adopting a donkey when needed and abandoning it when its use has expired is responsible for the large numbers of feral animals that abound today, particularly in North and South America, Asia and Australia. There are also many stranded on small islands in the Caribbean and Mediterranean, unwanted and short of food.

In Australia working donkeys ousted by farm machinery in the early twentieth century were turned loose and, in the same way as the rabbits introduced towards the end of the eighteenth century, flourished in such numbers that they soon became a pest. The first donkeys had been brought to Australia in 1794, when three arrived on board ship from Calcutta (three more having died during the journey). Subsequently they were imported in large numbers – Spanish stock via the USA, other types from India and South America – and being ideally suited to conditions in the outback they played a vital role in agriculture and development of the land. Although there were a few breeding programmes, most donkeys bred randomly: due to the variety of large breeds involved, particularly sturdy, tall specimens resulted. These, known as Teamsters, were used as draft animals in teams of up to thirty strong, and were remarkable for being driven by voice alone. As the need for draft animals declined, many of the Teamsters were abandoned and a feral breed evolved. Despite various government programmes which involved the shooting of tens of thousands of these feral donkeys, they continue to breed, and have also interbred with the smaller stock imported from England and Ireland in the 1970s, producing an Australian donkey population of wide variety but with no formal stud recognition. The problem of sheer numbers continues – an estimated five million feral donkeys now roam Australia's outback, grazing land which it is claimed is sorely needed by other, more profitable domestic animals. The most recent solution is to export them to China for human consumption via a 'processor' in Charleville, Queensland – a bitter reprisal for an animal that was pivotal in making the land fit for grazing in the first place, a century and a half earlier.

Even in such a hazy photograph, the majesty and size of the Australian Teamsters is unmistakable.

Donkeys were introduced to South America and Mexico by the Conquistadors in the sixteenth century. It was from Mexico, three centuries later, that they were imported to the western United States when Mexican prospectors flooded in on the optimistic wave of the gold rush. Burros were the ideal pack animals for this enterprise, carrying tools and camping equipment while prospecting went on, then working as haulage animals both in the mines and above ground. Later, as was so often the case once their usefulness was over, they were turned loose.

In North America, culling of feral donkeys is commonplace. A campaign to stop them being shot at Big Bend Ranch State Park in southern Texas by boycotting the park is currently in progress. Many of the shootings are brutal, with animals being wounded and left to die. The donkeys have lived on this 120,000 hectare desert wilderness for several hundred years, possibly ousting the big-horn sheep they had originally shared it with. The alleged reason for the shootings is the desire to reintroduce big-horned sheep, but this is seen as financially motivated since hunting the sheep is bigger business.

Big business too is the sale of the skins of feral donkeys to China for use as an ingredient in a traditional medicine that is meant to increase libido – women's specifically – and help with period pains. A deal for up to a million skins per year from the Northern Territory was being negotiated in 2008, an extraordinary number since there were then reckoned to be only 300,000 feral donkeys in the Territory. The Hong-Kong based company had previously obtained its donkey skins from South America. The skins were said to be worth the pitiful sum of $37 each. (Donkey skin, particularly that of wild donkeys, was used in ancient times to make both parchment and shoe leather.)

♦ ♦ ♦

Although our story lies with domesticated donkeys, no study of these would be complete without casting a glance at their wild relations, still called asses. And it is surely relevant to the donkey nature as we know it, that despite declining numbers these wild animals far outnumber those of any other domesticated species. The question of species is complex and disputed, and not something that needs to be addressed here, but since Africa is thought to be the cradle of both mankind and the donkey, this seems a good place to start.

As we have seen, the closest relatives to our domestic donkeys are the wild asses that originated in northeastern Africa, the species *Equus africanus*. The first subspecies was the Nubian, a small yellowish animal with a distinctive dark cross on back and shoulders that flourished throughout Egypt and the Sudan and was therefore probably the first to be domesticated. The second subspecies, the north African wild ass, is extinct. The third, the Somalian, most resembles the zebra. Taller than the Nubian, the Somali has a stiff upright mane and a smooth coat of pale grey or fawn, with white underbelly and legs; the legs are horizontally striped with black and the tail bears a zebra-like black tassel.

The African wild asses are swift as well as sure-footed and hardy, living in small groups on extremely arid land: they are reputed to be able to go without water for three days. Both subspecies of this tough breed are however on the critical list of species: the Nubian is thought to be extinct in the wild, and the Somali is declining rapidly, with only a few hundred in Somalia and a possible few thousand in Ethiopia. Many others are kept in zoos, mostly in North America and Europe; Basel Zoo has specialised in the Somali wild ass, having bred 35 in the last forty years.

The largest of the wild asses is the Kiang, sometimes called Tibetan, a native of the high, cold Tibetan plateau. In this dry climate the growing season for plants lasts only two to three months, so the animals must eat as much as they can during that time to put on fat to last the winter. They have particularly tough, thick lips, and the roof of their mouth is ridged to help them eat the rough grasses and shrubs that grow in this harsh habitat.

The Asian wild ass, *Equus hemionus*, is a different species with five subspecies, one of which, the Syrian wild ass, is extinct. These animals exist in a habitat that is harsh too, but at the other end of the scale: summer temperatures that can reach 50 degrees centigrade. Here finding water is the chief problem, and for this reason they live in larger herds than other asses, staying near any available water-holes for as long as they can. They have also adapted to eating low-growing plants and grasses, and may even when desperate eat salty soil. Onagers are strong as well as fast: they were recorded pulling chariots in the ancient Mesopotamian kingdom of Sumer as long ago as 2600 BC. (The Romans had a siege engine, a sort of giant catapult, called an onager, the name deriving from the fierce kicking action of the machine.) These asses are now found in Mongolia, Turkestan, Iran and Syria, but are on the IUCN Red List of threatened species. They are elegant animals, with honey-coloured coats and pale beige legs and underbelly; the upright, zebra-like mane is dark brown, and they have a brown dorsal stripe but without the 'cross' familiar to us. The Kulan, another subspecies of the Asian wild ass, once widespread over an immense region of the Gobi desert, now survives only in semi-desert steppe country in central Mongolia. The Indian wild ass, the Khur, is the fleetest of all, and claims are made for its being able to reach speeds of 70 kilometres an hour.

◆ ◆ ◆

Figures for these wild cousins of our domestic donkey are necessarily approximate, and there is a real danger of more becoming extinct, but some authorities are alarmist about the domestic donkey too. Despite the healthy numbers reported from China, Africa, India and elsewhere outside of Europe, a report published in 2007/2008 by the Swiss Monitoring Institute for Rare Breeds and Seeds in Europe declared: 'Not only are individual breeds endangered, the whole [donkey] species is heading for extinction!' The report provides an impressively thorough census of the different breeds and types of donkey throughout Europe, from Albania to the United Kingdom via Kosovo, Sweden and France. It gives the current numbers worldwide as 41 million, though falling – but surely still a long way from extinction.

The wild ass *Equus hemionus*, renowned for its hardiness and speed, here seen in the Gobi National Park, Mongolia.

And so the donkey lives on, as it has always done, in a variety of conditions and habitats, manmade and natural, tolerating extremes of terrain and temperature as it tolerates the vagaries of human expectation – from pampered pet to overworked drudge. To question this is to question the animal itself. This is how it is. The donkey asks no questions. The donkey *is*.

DONKEYS
of legend and fable

Aesop, the most legendary of legend-writers to whom the body of
Greek fables is ascribed, wrote in the sixth century BC and was
thought to have been a freed slave who would therefore probably have
had close contact with donkeys. It is therefore surprising that in most
of his fables that include donkeys they take on the stereotype of
stupidity. But in 'The Man, the Boy and the Donkey' it is the humans
that are made to look stupid, even though the donkey comes off badly
too. A man and his son are on the way to market, leading their
donkey. 'You idiots!' exclaims a fellow traveller. 'What's a donkey for
but to ride?' So the father puts his son on the donkey. 'See that lazy
boy, riding while his father walks,' comments a passer-by. So the two
change place. 'How can you make a young boy walk all that way?'
demands busybody number three, so of course the man climbs up to
join his son. All goes well until someone protests at their making the
poor donkey carry such a load. Stung by this latest criticism, the two
cut a pole, tie the donkey's feet to it, and carry the unfortunate animal
upside down – until they can go no further for the laughing, jeering
crowd. The donkey comes to a sad end, for while they are trying to
release him from the pole he is tipped over the side of a bridge and
drowned. 'Please all and you will please no one' is the moral of the tale.

Midas, king of Phrygia, is best associated in Greek myth for the gift,
granted by Dionysos, of being able to turn everything he touched into
gold – a power he begged to be relieved of when even his food was
affected. But Midas also has a donkey story. Asked to perform the
delicate task of adjudicating in a musical contest between the gods
Apollo and Pan, he chose the latter. Apollo, outraged, changed Midas's

ears into those of a donkey. Midas managed to conceal the ears from everyone but his barber, whom he swore to secrecy. The barber, burning with the secret but not daring to tell anyone, dug a hole in the ground and whispered his juicy piece of gossip into it. Thereafter whenever the wind blew, the reeds that had grown in the hole whispered the story to those passing by.

Donkeys play their part in the myth of Dionysos himself. In one story, Dionysos was riding into battle alongside Hephaestus and some satyrs, all of them on donkeys, against 'the giants'. (Precisely who or what these giants were remains obscure; an image of lots of Shreks comes to mind.) On their approach the donkeys set up a fearful braying, and the giants were so terrified by the noise that they upped sticks and fled. In gratitude, Dionysos named two stars in the constellation of Cancer after donkeys – Asini (sometimes Aselli) Borealis and Australis, i.e. north and south. The two stars are also called the Asses' Crib or Manger.

Dionysos, a modern reproduction of an ancient Greek wall plaque.

A lesser known story about Dionysos tells of him travelling to seek advice from his father's oracle for a fit of madness imposed on him by Hera, goddess of marriage and of women's sexuality. On the way he came to a swamp, impassable on foot. Determined to get across, he found a donkey which took him to the oracle – and his cure. He rewarded the animal by granting it the power of human speech. But this went to the donkey's head and he challenged the god Priapos on the size of their respective sexual organs. Not only did Priapos win – which says a lot for him – he then proceeded to kill the donkey for its impertinence. But Priapos already had a head of steam built up around the subject of donkeys: Ovid has three stories of the randy god, about to commit a rape, being foiled by the braying of a donkey.

Silenos, the foster-father of Dionysos, was the god of drunkenness and so seldom able to keep to his own feet that he is usually portrayed riding a donkey, which doubtless would have handled the excesses with its usual aplomb. A fourth-century BC coin from Mende depicts Dionysos seated on a donkey, facing backwards.

The Romans wrote about donkeys too. In one of Virgil's Unpublished Legends he has a donkey make an ass out of an enemy who had labelled him, Virgil, the ass. When the two men are seated with many others at the Emperor's table, Virgil offers to perform a 'merry jest' concerning a donkey the Emperor has given him. The donkey enters the banqueting hall and bows before the Emperor. 'He has come to visit his brother,' sniggers Virgil's enemy. 'That is true,' says the ass, and walking up to the man he wishes him good day. Furious, the unfortunate man tries to reply but all that comes out is a shattering bray. The more he brays the more the assembled company laugh, and it is some time before order is restored so that Virgil can press home his victory. 'Tell me, Ciuchino, my donkey, which of us three is the real ass? For your brother there says that I am one, and you call him brother, and yet from your appearance I would say that you are the one.' The wise donkey replies, 'Never trust outward appearances in this world. By their *voice* you shall know them . . .'

♦ ♦ ♦

The best fables bring out the essence of their subjects. The twentieth-century Guatemalan writer Augusto Monterroso was known for his quixotic animal fables (in Spanish, language of the quixotic). I particularly love this one. 'Flung into a field a long time ago, a Flute lay soundless, until one day a passing Donkey blew into it, bringing forth the sweetest sound of its life – that is to say, of the Donkey's life and the Flute's life too. Incapable of understanding what had happened, since rationality was not their forte and both believed in rationality, they hurriedly separated, abashed by this finest thing that either had ever done during its doleful existence.'

In his Literary Fables the Spanish poet Tomás de Iriarte captures the essence of donkey in the fewest possible words: 'There are donkeys plenty, / Who, without one jot of art, / May, for once, well play a part, / By chance.

There are asses in both the Old and New Testaments. The story of Balaam and his ass is well known, one of the earliest to present the donkey as being wiser than its master. Three times the ass avoids the avenging angel that Balaam cannot see, and three times it is beaten for its pains. Finally 'the Lord opened the mouth of the ass, and she said unto Balaam, What have I done unto thee, that thou hast smitten me these three times?. . . Am not I thine ass, upon which thou hast ridden ever since I was thine unto this day? Was I ever wont to do so unto thee?' A gut-wrenching cry echoed by donkeys without number down the ages.

The Holy Family's flight into Egypt and the Nativity both inspired a host of paintings featuring donkeys from the Middle Ages on, but two related legends are less well known. After their long exile in Egypt, Joseph decides to take the family back to Nazareth. At night they camp by the roadside. One night, while they are asleep, the donkey hears soldiers approaching on horseback. Sensing danger and trying to wake his owner, he neighs and neighs but the sound is too soft and the family sleep on. Desperate, the donkey prays to God for a loud voice – and hence came the bray, a bray like a dozen trumpets.

The donkey that bore Jesus into Jerusalem on Palm Sunday is said to have waited and followed Him to Calvary. Overcome by the sight the donkey turned away, but could not leave. As he stood there – we can imagine the characteristic droop – the shadow of the cross fell upon his back and shoulders, a lasting testimony to the animal's love and devotion.

'Jesus on the lean donkey, this is an emblem of how the rational intellect should control the animal-soul,' wrote the Persian poet Rumi.

A legend told to me by an Iranian one evening in Andalucía, when the wine flowed, names were forgotten and facts blurred, is too good not to relate despite the haziness. The story lays the responsibility for one stage of the prolonged war between the Persians and the Romans at the feet of a donkey. The Persian king – who has to remain nameless – was utterly devoted to his donkey, and when the animal mysteriously disappeared he was distraught. Search parties were sent out and huge rewards offered, all to no avail. The Roman commander, feeling for the Persian's distress through his devotion to a very special horse of his own, made an extraordinary (though clearly strategically motivated) offer: he would give him the horse. 'Not on your life,' replied the Persian. 'I wouldn't exchange one hair of my donkey for ten of your horses.' Predictably this was not well received and the war raged on; it lasted for over seven centuries, with the depressing result of 'status quo ante bellum', or back to square one. Certainly the white Hamadan donkeys from Persia are a breed to be proud of, some as big as a horse and still used in Iran and the USSR as riding animals.

It is no surprise that the Romans were of the high-horse brigade and looked down upon donkeys. An anecdote about the Emperor Hadrian makes this clear. One of his generals came to him seeking promotion and, putting his case, cited his many years of service in the army: 'I am very experienced. I have been in ten major battles.' Hadrian, who didn't think the general was qualified for a higher rank, waved his hand at some donkeys tethered nearby. 'My dear general, do you see those donkeys? Each has been in at last twenty battles, but all are still donkeys.'

A bizarre episode concerns a graffito scratched in plaster on a wall near the Palatine Hill in Rome. The crude cartoon shows a man gesturing at a crucified figure with the head of a donkey. The inscription, in Greek, identifies the man as a Roman soldier, Alexamenos, and can be translated either as 'Alexamenos worshipping God' or as a command, 'Alexamenos, worship God!'. Either way this strange image, probably dating from the beginning of the third century AD and therefore one of the earliest pictorial representations of the Crucifixion yet discovered, is a highly blasphemous caricature.

In Rome at this time donkeys were being used as bait, along with Christians, in the spectator sports held in the Colosseum. In AD 284, in the reign of Diocletian, fifty wild donkeys are recorded as having passed through in the course of one season of Games, along with such exotic beasts as elephants, lions, zebras and one lone rhinoceros.

But to right the balance just a little for the Romans, Jiménez pays them a compliment when he describes his donkey Platero as 'the Marcus Aurelius of the meadows', likening him to the philospher king for whom nature was a source of instruction and inspiration.

One of the names attributed to Muhammad's donkey – it seems he had many – was Barach (variously Barack or Borak), which means to kneel and therefore by implication to praise God. Barach was the subject of many fables and thought to possess extraordinary gifts, among them the ability to distinguish Jews from Muslims. He, or maybe it was Ya'foor, was also attributed with the power of speech, and was bold enough to address the Prophet himself. According to Shi'ite tradition this donkey committed suicide because he was frightened that on his master's death he would fall into the hands of someone who was not a prophet. Later on, the donkey became the preferred choice of mount for Muhammad's disciples who wanted, literally, to follow in his footsteps.

Donkeys often make an ass out of their owner in the stories concerning Nasreddin Hodja. Nasreddin, a thirteenth-century philospher and wit from Anatolia, was renowned from Greece to China for his simple anecdotes which often make him the fool. In one, he is asked, 'Hodja, why are you riding along bareback with your donkey's saddle on your shoulder?' 'It's because my poor old donkey was getting tired, so I thought I'd carry the saddle for him.' There is a miniature painting of Nasreddin wearing an enormous  confection of a turban which dwarfs both him and the donkey he is riding – potential for a similar joke, maybe.

In another tale Nasreddin agrees to deliver nine donkeys to a local farmer. Before he sets off, the owner counts them carefully so that there can be no mistake. On the road Nasreddin stops and, sitting astride one of the animals, counts them. He counts them again and again. He can only see eight! In a panic he jumps off, looks around and counts them once more. There are nine. After repeating this several times he notices that when he is sitting on one donkey he can see only eight, but as soon as he dismounts there are nine again. Being a good Mulla he thinks about the moral of this. 'It is the penalty for riding, when no doubt I should be walking behind the donkeys,' he concludes. So he sets off once more, walking behind the donkeys, and eventually they arrive at their destination. The farmer welcomes them and asks Nasreddin whether he has had any trouble on the way. 'No,' replies the Mulla. 'Once I had learned the trick of donkey-drivers, to walk behind, everything was fine. Before that, they were full of mischief.'

Nasreddin, a sort of medieval Mr Bean often depicted riding backwards on his donkey, usually manages to get the better of his opponents in the end. In another tale, a neighbour asks if he may borrow the Mulla's donkey. Nasreddin doesn't think much of this man, so he tells him that he has already lent the donkey to someone else. On overhearing this lie, the donkey brays loudly. Seemingly unembarrassed at being found out, Nasreddin demands of the indignant man, 'Whom would you rather believe, a donkey or your Mulla?'

Many of the Christian saints have donkey stories to tell. St Francis, patron saint of all animals, is thought to have travelled the pilgrim's road to Santiago de Compostela between 1213 and 1215, though there is some dispute about this. If he did, he would most probably have taken the northern route around the Mediterranean to Barcelona, founding monasteries as he went. Though he walked for much of the way, he was believed also to have taken a donkey. Maybe this was what prompted the saint's remark that a man should treat his body as he treats his donkey. An interesting observation, and one that we would do well to observe since today there are probably even more ill-treated human bodies than there are ill-treated donkeys. But the most charming legend is that on his deathbed St Francis thanked his donkey for carrying him and helping him throughout his life, and the donkey wept. For our argument, it is the 'helping him' that is especially significant.

St Anthony, a Franciscan in whom St Francis himself took a particular interest, is the patron saint specifically of donkeys and horses – as well as of lost things. One day St Anthony was challenged by a Jewish merchant to prove the 'fable' of the holy Eucharist. In a contest devised by the merchant, a donkey was starved for three days, while the saint retreated to a forest to fast and pray for three days. When he returned to town he went to the church where he obtained the Blessed Sacrament, and then to the town square where the donkey was. A bale of hay was placed some metres from the hungry animal. As it walked towards the hay, St Anthony held out the monstrance and called to the donkey, 'In the name of the Lord our God, I command you to come here and worship your Creator!' The donkey stopped, turned and walked to St Anthony. It then bent its forelegs, bowing to the ground before the Blessed Sacrament. The astonished merchant asked for forgiveness and was converted.

St Nicholas, born in a small village on what is now the southern coast of Turkey, was revered for his support of the needy and oppressed long before he became known as Santa Claus. He was tall and thin, and wore the dress of a bishop, a red habit and mitred hat; only the long white beard we now associate with him was original. In parts of Europe Santa Claus was thought to have ridden a white horse when doing his Christmas rounds, but in France, Belgium and Switzerland he was often portrayed, more aptly for a champion of the underdog, walking alongside a donkey laden with presents – or even riding it, as in this Christmas card.

From this comes another legend: the origin of Pfeffernüsse, small spiced biscuits traditionally eaten at Christmas in Germany and Scandinavia. The story goes that St Nicholas left his donkey outside a church while he went in to worship, and when he came out the donkey had disappeared. The saint enlisted the help of some nearby fishermen, who blew cow horns to lure the donkey back. The search continued until at last, from far away through the snow that had now begun to fall, there came an answering bray. Slowly, in the way that so many donkey owners will recognise, the animal appears out of the gloom 'like a vision'; he is led back to his master by a group of children, and it is easy to imagine him ambling over and wondering what all the fuss is about. But the climax of this strange story comes when amid all the excitement at his return the donkey, who obviously had found good grazing in the course of his adventure, begins to drop 'the fruits of his digestion' on the freshly fallen snow. Miraculously, these turn out to be – not droppings but 'rich, round, spicy Pfeffernüsse'.

A fable from the North American Sioux tells of a grandmother, wife of the chief, who made two saddle bags for her twin grandsons, and brought along a donkey. 'He is patient and surefooted. He shall carry the babes in the saddle bags, one on either side of his back.' But the boys' father did not think a donkey good enough for his sons and one day, when he and the chief's daughter were going on a journey with the boys, he led out his finest pony and put the saddle bags on its back. 'There, my sons shall ride on a pony, not on a donkey; let the donkey carry the pots and pans.' The donkey didn't think much of this, and as soon as he had been loaded with all the household goods he began to kick and rear and bray, breaking everything in sight and causing mayhem. They rushed to the grandmother, who laughed. 'Did I not tell you the donkey was for the children? He knows they are the chief's grandsons, so do you think he will be content to carry pots and pans?' They set off, with the donkey quietly carrying the twins in their saddle bags. But the following day the party was attacked and a violent battle took place. When finally the chief's family had defeated the marauders, they looked round – and there was no donkey. Having searched in vain they returned miserably to their village and there, in front of the grandmother's tepee, was the donkey with his precious cargo safe and sound.

Gypsies have long been associated with donkeys, and according to one story the animals played a key role in gypsy history. Although there is some argument as to where gypsies originated, the most common claim is that it was in northwest India. The story goes that Bahram V, king of Persia in the early fifteenth century, was upset that his poorer subjects were unable to afford the necessary fees for musicians to play during their festivals. So he wrote to his brother-in-law, ruler of a kingdom in northern India, asking him to send musicians. According to who tells the story, ten to twelve thousand musicians – a lot of music either way – duly arrived and were given donkeys, cows and seedcorn so that they could feed themselves in return for playing for the poor free of charge. A year later the musicians returned to Bahram with the donkeys, starving. They had been so happy playing music that they hadn't bothered to cultivate the land, and had first eaten the corn, then the cows; only the donkeys remained. The king, furious, told them to go off with their donkeys and travel the world, earning their living by music. He did not add by scrounging and thieving but unfortunately that is a reputation, however undeserved, that gypsies have found it hard to live down.

The contemporary Indian poet Suniti Namjoshi weaves a story around Chagall's Blue Donkey and then makes her the protagonist in *The Blue Donkey Fables*, most of which feature animals. The opening story has the Blue Donkey, as portrayed by Chagall, in a field next to a red bridge. The town councillors object that this is inartistic. 'A donkey who lives by our bright red bridge must be of the purist and silkiest white or we must request that the said donkey be required to move on.'

It soon turns into a political issue, with one party prepared to accept a compromise if the donkey becomes a nondescript grey, while the other claims that this imposes a slur on the donkey's ability to achieve whiteness. 'Good heavens!' cried the others. 'Are you suggesting that the donkey's blueness may be a matter of culpable wilfulness rather than a mere genetic mischance?' (Or an artist's whim, we might add.) So they decide to consult the donkey. They present their case: go grey or move on. 'Can't and won't,' replies the donkey, living up to the stubborn stereotype before turning the tables. 'I'm a perfectly good donkey,' she said at last. 'What exactly is the matter with you?' When they explain that they are troubled by her blueness, but can't agree what to do, her advice is 'Look again.' Which they do, and soon get used to her colour, though the opposing parties maintain their difference of opinion. But 'there were still a few others who managed to see . . . that the Blue Donkey was only herself and therefore beautiful. These last occasionally brought her a bunch of blue flowers which she put in a vase.'

Word gets round and people flock to see her, and for a while she basks in her fame. But being sensitive she soon wearies of tourists and the trappings of fame (bars, bistros and trinkets), and her coat, chopped at by souvenir hunters, becomes scruffy and grey. She decides to retire. The townsfolk are horrified. 'But what about us? What can we possibly tell the tourists?' 'Tell them the truth. Tell them that I have become a legend,' she replies grandly. 'But will it work?' 'Of course,' she assures them. 'Truth is dazzling.'

In her retirement the Blue Donkey comes to be revered by the other animals as poet and even saint and sought out for her wise pronouncements, but she is not very comfortable with this – she sees herself as just an ordinary creature and besides, she has endearing faults which include a vulgar streak. So when at the end of the book she is wrong-footed and humiliated by a caterpillar and slinks away feeling 'uselesss, hopeless and utterly snubbed', our hearts go with her.

Jeanette Winterson, in her part of a serial story written by four different authors, has a donkey say: 'When I was carrying Mary to Bethlehem, you'll recall that it was for a census. Everyone had to be counted. But in all that counting the one thing that couldn't be counted was the one thing that changed everything. Mary was carrying a child. Not what was measured but what was smuggled in turned out to be the miracle. By which I mean, and I should know, that you can plan and order as much as you like, but where life rips at the seams is where love is let in.' *And I should know.* Identifying the donkey with pain, and with love, seems to come naturally.

◆ ◆ ◆

Because of their usefulness as pack animals as well as their stoic qualities under taxing conditions, donkeys have always played a part in warfare. A story from the First World War concerns Jack Simpson, acclaimed as 'Australia's best-loved military hero'. Born Jack Simpson Kirkpatrick in 1892 at South Shields, on the north-east coast of England, he had worked as a donkey boy on the beaches there before setting off in 1910 to seek his fortune in Australia. Having taken a series of unsatisfactory jobs on sea and land, when he heard of the outbreak of war in 1914 Simpson got himself enlisted in the Australian Army and became a field ambulance stretcher-bearer. On 25 April his unit landed in Gallipoli, on a savage piece of Turkish coast now known as Anzac Cove.

The next day, carrying casualties back to cover over his shoulder, Simpson saw a donkey. For the following twenty-four days, ignoring a steady barrage from artillery, field guns and snipers, he trudged the two kilometres between beach and front line, night and day, with a series of donkeys – Duffy, Murphy and Abdul – carrying

Jack Simpson (centre) with one of the donkeys that helped him to save so many lives at Gallipoli.

over 300 wounded men to safety. Simpson's charmed life came to an end on 19 May with a machine-gun bullet in the back; the donkey continued its journey bearing a wounded soldier, and then guided men back to the body. The story quickly gained mythical status: Simpson and 'the donkey' – which one appears to be irrelevant – were lauded and commemorated in no fewer than five sculptures, as well as on Australian postage stamps and medallions. Less fêted – though the subject of a well-known painting by Horace Moore-Jones thought originally to have been of Simpson – was Richard Alexander Henderson, a New Zealand private who continued the rescue mission with one of the donkeys after Simpson's death (see illustration p.23).

The use of donkeys in contemporary warfare takes a grisly turn in Afghanistan. In 2009, a donkey tethered to a tree south of Garmsir in the province of Helmand was used as a suicide bomber, its panniers packed with explosives. Miraculously no one except the poor donkey was killed when they were detonated, which may be why 'it wasn't long before the first donkey jokes started to come out – "drop the dead donkey" was one,' recorded a British officer. ('Drop the Dead Donkey' was the title of a Channel 4 comedy series in the 1990s – it being the story rather than the donkey that was to be dropped. An old saying has it that no one ever sees a dead donkey, which is why perhaps it is also considered very lucky to do so.)

Luck was not in evidence in another contemporary war story. Two small girls, searching for food with their donkey and cart in a small town in the northern Gaza Strip, were targeted by an Israeli 'intelligent' bomb and blown to pieces.

◆ ◆ ◆

If medicinal cures cannot quite be classed as legends, some old wives' tales concerning donkeys are worth recording. Hair cut from the cross on the back (and even dark donkeys are said to bear this) would be placed in a bag and hung round a child's neck in order to ward off fits, while hairs from the tail of a donkey were thought to alleviate afflictions as varied as whooping cough and scorpion stings. For the latter, a Jewish remedy published in AD 1400 was more specific: 'If a man who is riding a donkey is bitten by a scorpion, turns around and faces the donkey's tail, the pain will leave him and go to the donkey.' Both Hippocrates and Pliny prescribed asses' milk for the treatment of fevers, ulcers and asthma, and as a neutraliser against poison. In Africa it is still used in witchcraft remedies. Cosmetic rather than medicinal was the practice of bathing in asses' milk, attributed to such notorious lovers as Cleopatra, Poppaea, second wife of Nero, and Joséphine Bonaparte. Whether Napoleon's much quoted instruction, delivered to Joséphine a few days before his return from some campaign, '*Je reviens, ne lave pas,*' applied also to an asses' milk bath is not recorded.

A persistent, and probably true, donkey legend comes from Spain. In the 1950s the gypsies of Seville were hounded out of Triana, their traditional quarter in the city, and rehoused in a vast complex of tower blocks where they would not offend the sensibilities of the respectable Sevillanos. An old gypsy man in a new ninth-floor flat, who still worked his donkey (or mule, according to who tells the story) and grazed it on the remaining grass verges during the day, was uncertain what to do with it at night. So he turned the spare room into a stable and took the animal up in the lift every evening.

A hard-to-believe contemporary donkey story originated in 1987 from an article in *The Times* in which an 'expert' claimed that more people were killed by donkeys annually than died in commercial plane crashes. Whether the so-called expert worked for an airline is not known, but the story is passed on – along with the many other uncorroborated claims that turn into 'legends' through the Internet.

Lastly a modest legend of my own, born of my habit of walking my donkey in and around the Spanish village near which I used to live. One day I asked a driver at the bus station in Seville, over a hundred kilometres away, whether his bus stopped at X, a different village where I had left my car that morning. 'Yes,' he replied, 'but don't you want to go to Y?' I looked at him with astonishment. How could he possibly know where I lived? 'Well,' he said with a smile. 'You're the donkey lady, aren't you.'

CHAPTER 7

DONKEYS
in literature

The extremes so noticeable with regard to the donkey's character, and the layman's perception of the animal in general, apply equally to how it is portrayed in literature and art. On the one hand the doleful, sentimentalised Eeyore bumbling around with Pooh and Piglet, on the other donkeys being pitched upside down in the Donkey-Drowner river hurtling beneath the town of Antioch in Russell Hoban's *Pilgermann*: from Disney to Bosch. Or the dignified, noble beast of the New Testament, carefully bearing his precious burdens of the Virgin Mary and the condemned Christ, in contrast to the picture-postcard joker being dragged along the beach by a gang of hooligans. The only thing these caricatures have in common is the long-suffering nature of the donkeys concerned.

That donkeys have for so long featured, if not prominently but consistently, in both art and literature is not only because they were until the arrival of the motor the principal beast of burden, and therefore an integral part of daily life, but also I like to think because of their strong character.

The earliest known written reference to donkeys appears on a tablet from Nippur, in Mesopotamia, from the Old Babylonian Period, *c.*1900 BC. Here, among a list of wild and domestic animals in cuneiform, are two words for donkey, transliterated as *anše* and *dusu*.

Herodotus, the father of history who wrote in the fifth century BC, recounts how Xerxes, having entered Europe at the head of the Persian army, received two omens, one of which was that a horse gave birth to a hare, the other that a donkey gave birth to a foal that had both male and female genitals. Xerxes chose to ignore the omens and his army was defeated at the battle of Salamis.

An ass takes the eponymous role in what is considered to be the oldest surviving novel, a picaresque tale from the second century BC by the Roman writer and orator Lucius Apuleius. *The Golden Ass* (or *Metamorphoses*) is witty, boisterous and sexually explicit. Its hero, also called Lucius, is changed into a donkey after he offends a witch by having an affair with her slave-girl. During his 'spell' as an ass he undergoes many adventures, being beaten, chased by dogs and stolen. Tiring of all this, he is finally returned to human form after the Queen of Heaven appears to him in a vision and tells him to eat a bunch of roses held by one of her priests in a religious procession. He then becomes a disciple of the goddess Iris. Whether Apuleius knew donkeys at first hand is doubtful, for no self-respecting donkey will ever allow itself to be chased by a dog, though the rose-eating is spot on. *The Golden Ass* was admired by many Renaissance writers, and may have given Shakespeare the idea for Bottom's transformation into an ass in *A Midsummer Night's Dream*.

Although Bottom is a lovable ass he is still a figure of fun, and Titania's infatuation with him turns to disgust as soon as she is released from her spell. Elsewhere Shakespeare follows the stereotypical use of the word 'ass' as synonymous with stupidity – Dogberry, the constable in *Much Ado*

Benjamin Britten's *A Midsummer Night's Dream*, the 2006 Glyndebourne Festival Opera production with Íride Martínez as Titania and Matthew Rose as Bottom.

About Nothing, no less than three times – while the 'fool', professional jester and clown, is afforded considerable respect. (Writing in the early nineteenth century, Robert Surtees observed that 'Major Yammerton was rather a peculiar man, inasmuch as he was an ass, without being a fool.')

Pioneer in so many ways, Cervantes (who died in the same year as Shakespeare, 1616) was the first to attribute personalities to his animal characters – though thankfully he fell well short of anthropomorphism. Rather, the two mounts of the protagonists in *Don Quixote* reflect the characters of their owners: the skinny, gangly, aristocratic mare Rocinante and the rounded, bustling, cheerful Dapple are mirrors of the Don and his faithful servant Sancho Panza. Coleman Barks, translator of Rumi and himself a mercurial wordsmith, coins the adjective 'panzaic' as a complement to quixotic: 'No gaunt, bookish savior of damsels, the panzaic rider smells of donkey and spilled beer. He's commonsensical, ambitious for himself and family, earthy, and very loyal in his friendship' – a description that fits Dapple, or any other donkey, just as well as it does his master.

This engraving by Gustave Doré captures perfectly the anguished remorse of Sancho Panza and Dapple's resigned acceptance of his master's folly.

The eighteenth-century French philosopher, poet and wit Voltaire, giving instructions for what he wanted as a frontispiece for *The Ignorant Philosopher*, wrote modestly: 'The thing is to represent three blind men who grope after a fleeing donkey. This is the symbol of all philosophers who run after the truth. I consider myself one of the blindest, and have always run after my donkey. So it is my portrait for which I am asking you.' Anyone who, fully sighted, has chased a fleeing donkey will recognise the power of this metaphor.

The donkey's bray as shock treatment for Dostoevsky's Prince Myshkin, the 'idiot' of the book's title, is elegantly explored by Andy Merrifield, who goes on to link it with Janov's primal scream. Well worth reading. There is too an obvious association to be made between the innocence combined with instinctive acuity of the so-called idiot and that of the 'silly ass'. Beneath the labels and the type-casting lies something very different.

Benjamin, the old donkey in *Animal Farm*, plays a typically backstage yet significant part in Orwell's allegory of political corruption. Enclosed and resigned, he sees everything but says nothing, merely nodding his muzzle with a knowing air. He remains sceptical of the revolution being staged on the farm by his comrades and for the most part keeps out of the action, declining to take sides when the animals begin to fall out. But when his friend Boxer, the horse, collapses from overwork and is about to be taken off to 'hospital', it is Benjamin who reacts violently and tries to warn the others that in fact his friend is being taken to the knacker's yard. Just as it is he who reads out the book's most chilling message, the central dénouement, ALL ANIMALS ARE EQUAL BUT SOME ANIMALS ARE MORE EQUAL THAN OTHERS. Benjamin's faithful attachment to Boxer, his low-key wisdom, his refusal to meddle, his long-term memory are all in character, as is his sudden and unexpected action in a genuine crisis. This is donkey nature well portrayed.

The donkey used as a working animal, with little consideration from its keepers, is commonly portrayed in fiction. 'No one really has any idea how much an ass can take. A hundred pounds? Two hundred? Half a dozen sacks of rice? Three kegs of gunpowder and a crate of walnut-framed mirrors in the Queen Anne style? A roll of baft the size of a giant redwood? There is no question that the creature is a beast of burden, that it exists to haul things as surely as a mosquito exists to draw blood,' writes T.C. Boyle of an early nineteenth-century expedition in search of the source of the river Niger.

Describing the digging of a two-kilometre tunnel beneath Lake Ontario, Michael Ondaatje tells how the mules used for transporting the excavated soil below ground were lowered down the shaft by rope, their

Overloading the ass is as old as the story of mankind's use of him, whether in Pakistan or Persia. The one on the right is a Hamadan, photographed in Tabriz, home of Rumi's great friend Shams.

legs bound to prevent them injuring themselves. There they stayed until they died or the tunnel reached its goal. 'And when would that be? The brain of the mule no more nor less knowledgeable than the body of a man who dug into a clay wall in front of him.' (Although ponies were the usual choice for working in mines, particularly in England, mules and donkeys were also used, the latter particularly where the shafts were very low.) Ondaatje also mentions the steam donkey, a small steam engine usually used as an auxiliary on board ship, though in this case as part of the pumping equipment for the tunnel.

Less harsh, though only narrowly avoiding the sentimental, is Paul Gallico's *The Small Miracle*, a small book about a small boy and his donkey. Pepino is an orphan with 'enormous dark eyes, large ears, and close-cropped, upstanding hair' – a description which could well have fitted Violetta, his donkey. The two of them scratch a living in Assissi by fetching and carrying and doing odd jobs. Violetta is his heritage and his livelihood, as well as his best friend. When one day Violetta falls ill and the vet fails to cure her, Pepino decides that the only hope is to take her to the crypt where the remains of St Francis are buried.

Here predictably he comes up against ecclesiastical hypocrisy as church officials huff and puff at the thought of a donkey being let into the crypt. Tut, tut, what an idea. But Pepino, undeterred, takes out his precious savings, pays a friend to look after Violetta, and sets off for Rome. Here, with the help of a bunch of lilies-of-the-valley and a heart-stirring note, he works his way up the hierarchy until he is in the presence of the Pope himself. His Holiness – predictably too, but how relieved one is that he at last is sympathetic – agrees that Pepino must be allowed to take his donkey to see the saint, and Pepino returns with letters of authorisation for Violetta to be allowed into the crypt. This entails the breaking down of an old walled-up door, in the course of which a small leaden box is revealed with 'the year 1226, when St Francis died, engraved on the side, and the large initial "F".' Whether this, or the presumed curing of Violetta, is the small miracle of the title we are left to decide for ourselves.

The Small Miracle, drawing by Edgar Norfield.

Another small book about a boy and a donkey has a very different flavour. In *Isfendiar and the Wild Donkeys*, written sixteen years after *The Small Miracle* in 1967, the hero is a charcoal-burner's son from a village on the edge of the desert in southern in Iran. He is obsessed by the idea that there remain descendants of the wild donkeys that had once ranged the harsh land between the Himalayas and the Mediterranean before being hunted by man to make shoe leather from their skin. 'And the years and the centuries and the ages of the desert that were in the eternal tapestry of the Iranian sky were all a part of them, of the fleet wild donkeys.' Like Pepino, Isfendiar persuades someone to look after things in his absence – in this case, to herd the family goats – and sets off alone on his mission. He crosses the desert and comes to the salt flats, but by the third day he is still far from the mountains where he hopes to find the wild asses. Overcome by thirst and weariness he lies down, accepting that he has failed and will surely die. His salvation comes in the form of a Jeep carrying three men, 'foreigners, from the north' who are exploring the desert. Despite the hostility of one of them, Isfendiar captures the imagination of the other two with his description of the wild donkeys – 'the rarest of the rare, the noblest animal ever to walk on the earth, the animal of which the great poets speak' – and they agree to take him to the mountains and help him in his search.

At last they find the herd of donkeys, and the boy manages to snare a young colt, '. . . the prettiest animal Isfendiar had ever seen. It had noble russet, gray and peach coloring, with sepia mane and markings on its tail. The belly was the pearliest white. Its eyes stared, unfrightened, at the group around it.' They set off for home with the colt rather improbably lodged in the back of the Jeep, to be greeted by the village elder. But here the story takes a surprising turn, far from the 'boy and donkey live happily ever after' that Westerners might expect. Isfendiar, who has come of age in the desert, decides that the donkey must be taken to 'the city', Teheran, where it will be kept in a zoo and appreciated by many, while he gets on with the work for which he is now fit, in his father's kiln. The book ends with Isfendiar's proud words: 'For now I am a charcoal-burner and can see the perfection of creation.'

Moving from the Persian desert to the Provençal countryside, *L'Âne Culotte* is an allegorical tale of animals, dark magic and an earthly paradise complete with serpent. The book sprang from stories told by Henri Bosco, a French schoolmaster from Avignon, to his 'fat and lovely' pupils – imagine saying that today – whom he thought needed a bit of fantasy as well as some Provençal sunlight in the 'drab, rainy, isolated village' where he was then teaching. Published in 1937 the book quickly became a runaway success; it was much admired by André Gide, who was said to prefer it to *Le Grand Meaulnes*.

Henri Bosco knew about donkeys from his childhood. The donkey Culotte is 'an unobtrusive donkey . . . a donkey that certainly loved

reflection; a donkey that had seen much, retained much in his lifetime
. . . a donkey endowed with a soul.' But a sense of the ridiculous
shatters this rather too perfect image when we learn that this donkey
wears trousers, brown corduroy trousers (front legs only) held up by
leather suspenders. How this came about we never quite understand,
and the next time we meet Culotte he is transformed, 'no longer a
donkey of this earth, a village burro . . . He was the enchanted donkey,
the magic donkey. . . . He stepped forward from the depths of donkey
history, laden with all the legends about donkeys that can possibly
spread throughout the world.' I love these contrasts: the ordinary
village burro, the figure of fun in his trousers, and the mythical being
carrying all of donkey history on his back.

In *The Donkey Who Always Complained* (a misleading title) Francis B.
Thornton personifies the donkeys that carried Mary to Bethlehem,
helped the family flee to Egypt, witnessed miracles and finally carried
Jesus into Jerusalem on Palm Sunday. The tale is told to a group of her
friends by Balo, descendant of the donkey who bore the pregnant
Mary, who then herself witnesses Christ's crucifixion and is rewarded
with the sign of the cross on her back. Despite the sometimes purple
prose, the story has a steady pace that draws one along on this
familiar journey, told from a new angle.

◆ ◆ ◆

The donkey as travelling companion has long been a favourite subject
in literature and legend. From the Persian mystics to R.L. Stevenson,
from Sancho Panza to Juan Ramón Jiménez, donkey owners and
handlers, professionals and novices, have cursed or celebrated their
relationship with their cussed or cooperative beasts.

Stevenson's initial trials and tribulations with his put-upon little
donkey, and their eventual reconciliation, have already been told.
Setting out to follow in the exact footsteps of his fellow-countryman
and hero figure over a century later, Christopher Rush appears to
have had no relationship at all with his donkey, Anatole – indeed he
treats it more like a bicycle, 'parking' it for the night at the back of a
hotel between two Citroëns and failing to make a single observation
about the animal's character, nature or habits until one night, lost in

a fog and surrounded by trigger-happy *chasseurs*, the donkey kicks up his heels and disappears off into the dark. This does the trick: 'For the first time in the Cévennes I realized how much I'd come to depend on Anatole, not just as a porter but as a companion.' In the witchy way of donkeys, Anatole turns up, a 'docile shadowgraph of donkey materializing in the mist', and Rush in his relief – all his possessions having been in panniers on the donkey – greets him effusively, *'Veux-tu m'épouser? Tu es très joli! Je t'aime!'* But we are not fooled. This is a donkey-user not a donkey-lover in the mould of Rumi's Sufi (p.87), and even when Rush follows Stevenson in 'yielding to his emotion' at the moment of farewell, the tears seem to me if not downright crocodilian at least more to do with regret for the ending of a shared journey than with genuine affection for the animal.

Rush does however have some good things to say about travel. His own journey was undertaken as a kill or cure for destructive, all-consuming grief at the death of his wife. How many of the world's great pilgrimages, to Mecca, to Jerusalem, to Santiago de Compostela, are made from motives of loss, whether of a loved one or of the meaning of life? The essence of therapeutic travel is solitariness, and this is where the donkey as companion, carrier of man's emotional as well as literal baggage, comes into its own. St Francis, traveller extraordinary, who likened his body to a donkey (p.68), extended the metaphor to the body as faithful donkey accompanying the soul on its journey through life. Be kind to it therefore, he urges.

Tim Moore's long-suffering donkey, apart from carrying his physical luggage for over 750 kilometres across the north of Spain on the Santiago pilgrim's route, provided most of the laughs – and occasionally had the last one – in the author's relentless pursuit of what the blurb calls his 'rare comic talent'. This desire to have a laugh at the expense of donkeys used to make me feel protective, even indignant, until I came to see it as a gift that presupposes character. Laughter is preferable to scorn or pity, and donkeys so often give as good as they get that one cannot feel sorry for them for long. This is yet one more service they provide to man.

A modern traveller attuned to his donkey companion in a way that seems never to have occurred to Rush or Moore is Andy Merrifield. In *The Wisdom of Donkeys* he and his borrowed donkey, Gribouille (the Scribbler), meander through the countryside of central France, much as R.L. Stevenson had done more than a hundred years earlier, though for a longer and more demanding walk – and with considerably more pleasure for both man and beast. Yes, Merrifield uses the donkey as a literary device, just as Jiménez had done, talking to him, naming him frequently so that one is aware of his presence, bringing him into his internal conversations. In Merrifield's case the donkey acts as a sounding-board for his thoughts, therapist for a spirit exhausted by city life and the pursuit of power turned to dust, as a means even towards self-knowledge and enlightenment. But in all this there is no sense of exploitation, no sentimentality or toe-curling anthropomorphism, just a gently evolving sense of mutual trust and affection.

In his pursuit of what Merrifield calls 'passive adventuring' (after the French writer Pierre Mac Orlan), he and Gribouille scribble their way across the Auvergne, stopping often, talking to anyone they encounter, but mostly communing between each other as the pace, the peace and the countryside work their magic. But this is not just a country idyll, and in the course of this delightful book the author takes us from his native Liverpool to New York and back to rural France via many literary and artistic byways in the traditional donkey manner, zigzagging, pausing and pondering as the spirit moves them both.

One of the best-loved fictional donkeys in the West must be Eeyore in A.A. Milne's Pooh Bear stories. Though Eeyore is a caricature, he nevertheless does carry an essence of donkeyness which probably still colours many adult perceptions of the donkey, such as his laid-back quality and melancholy air. 'We can't all, and some of us don't,' says Eeyore. 'Can't all *what?*' asks Pooh. 'Gaiety. Song-and-dance . . . Bon-hommy.'

Eeyore, drawing by E.H. Shepard.

Long before his success with *Shrek* in 1990, William Steig had written and illustrated a children's story called *Sylvester and the Magic Pebble*. Sylvester the donkey, who makes a habit of collecting pebbles, one day comes across a pebble that grants wishes. When he is threatened by a lion, Sylvester impulsively asks the pebble to turn him into a rock. As is often the case with spells the problem is then how to undo it, a task which takes up the rest of the tale. And as in *Animal Farm* pigs play a key role, here as police – which caused the book to be banned in parts of the US, but didn't stop it being awarded the country's prestigious Caldecott Medal in 1970.

Names chosen for fictional animals, in our case donkeys, are worth observing. Why Sylvester? Or Benjamin? Eeyore we can understand, Platero and Gribouille. C.S. Lewis's choice of name for the donkey in the final Narnia story, *The Last Battle*, is Puzzle, an inspired choice for an animal both puzzled and puzzling. That this Puzzle is self-deprecating and possibly a bit simple doesn't detract from his character, and he plays his part in allowing himself to be used by the manipulative and also aptly named ape, Shift. In order to do so, Shift has Puzzle dress up in a lion's skin – surely the oldest trick in the book.

How different they are these donkeys, factual and fictional, loved, used and berated. Yet the thread of common donkeyness is there, weaving their stories together as they plod, and only occasionally kick up their heels in protest, along the hazardous path between the expectations of humans and their own needs as animals.

CHAPTER 8

DONKEYS
in poetry

Donkeys appear in poetry down the ages, sometimes taking an uncharacteristically prominent role, and far more frequently it seems than most other animals. Probably their first appearance goes back to 30 BC when Virgil wrote his poems about rural life, the *Georgics*, where he describes an ass being loaded up with apples and oil to take to market, to bring back the rather strange cargo of 'a dented mill-stone or black lump of pitch'.

Being particularly well endowed, male donkeys have often been the subject of sexual fantasies, from Apuleius on. The thirteenth-century Sufi poet Rumi, an earthy mystic for whom nothing was taboo in his bubbling celebration of the life-force, wrote graphically about a maidservant who devised a way of allowing a donkey to perform the services of a man without coming to harm herself. The servant's mistress, who has secretly watched 'the animal's marvelous member and the delight of the girl', decides she wants some of this for herself. So she sends her maid off on a long errand and presents herself to the donkey – with disastrous results, for she has not learned 'the importance of gourdcrafting', the poem's title.

Donkeys appear throughout Rumi's poetry, in many different situations and guises. More than once he associates the donkey with the human heart. Describing a despairing state of mind, he says, 'And my heart, I'd say it was more like a donkey sunk in a mudhole, struggling and miring deeper.' In 'You Sweep the Floor' he praises the 'heart-donkey' for its strength in leading the lover to his beloved. 'After the Meditation' tells the tale of a visiting Sufi who, rising in the evening from his meditation, remembers the donkey that has carried him faithfully all day. With touching attention to detail, he enquires about the care his animal will receive overnight. 'I want to make sure that you wet the barley first. He's an old donkey, and his teeth are shaky. . . . did you remove the saddle gently, and put salve on the sore he has? And did you currycomb his back? He loves that.' Having been assured by a smarmy servant that all these things are being seen to, the Sufi retires for the night. But once asleep he has nightmares about the donkey, dreaming that it is being savaged by a wolf, and falling into a ditch. Sure enough he wakes to find that the poor donkey has been sorely neglected and left without food and water all night. The moral is 'Do the careful, donkey-tending work. Don't trust that to anyone else. There are hypocrites who will praise you, but who do not care about the health of your heart-donkey.' The 'heart-donkey' seems to me a metaphor not only beautiful but apt: that small, robust organ, oblivious to its host but quietly getting on with its job, pumping away day after day, doing a lifetime's donkey work.

'Poor little Foal of an oppressed race', wrote Samuel Taylor Coleridge in a tender poem about a young donkey standing beside its tethered and hungry mother. Coleridge knew about dulled spirits and fears; he himself was an outsider, separated from his family as a child and suffering bouts of anxiety and depression throughout his troubled life.

Juan Ramón Jiménez was already an acclaimed poet when, at the age of twenty-six and suffering from the mental illness that dogged his life also, he began what was to become his most popular work, *Platero y Yo* (Platero and I). In this long prose-poem, which covers a year and is centred upon his small hometown in Andalucía and the surrounding countryside, the author uses the donkey as a fictional companion and sounding board. ('Platero' means silversmith – 'He's got pluck, there's steel in him. Steel and moon-silver at the same time' – though the descriptions of this donkey are probably a combination of all the ones Jiménez had known as a child.) Together he and Platero wander and observe. Unlike so many travellers with donkeys, Jiménez is not in a hurry. 'Platero nibbles the sparse grass of the shady banks, the dusty blossoms of the mallows, the yellow sorrel. He halts more than he walks. I let him.'

If at times Jiménez indulges in purple passages and verges on the anthropomorphic, his knowledge of and affection for donkeys, real or fictitious, is palpable. Whether it is Platero leaning on his shoulder ('Something huge and warm suddenly protrudes over my shoulder, like a living prow'), or eating, drinking, braying, greeting other donkeys – this is a donkey lovingly observed. Some of the images are unforgettable. In moonlight Platero 'breaks into a trot, enters the stream, treads on the moon, and shatters it to bits. It's as if a swarm of bright crystal roses were twining around his trotting legs, seeking to hold him back.' And though one would like to forget the story of the colt with his iridescent black coat prancing unaware to his fate of castration and emerging 'like a disbound book', it will not go away.

This, and the unsparing description of young Platero's sudden death from 'some venomous root', are doubtless some of the original stories that were deemed unsuitable when the first version of *Platero y Yo* was published, for children, in 1914. The first complete edition, double the number of chapters, followed three years later. With the rise of Franco in 1936 Jiménez left Spain, spending most of the rest of his life in America. In 1956, two years before he died, he was awarded the Nobel Prize for Literature.

Platero y Yo: La Autopsia, watercolour by Jesús Gabán.

Walter de la Mare, a contemporary of Jiménez, gives a contrasting and very English view of the donkey in his poem 'Nicholas Nye'. Tender and simple enough to be read to (and by) quite small children, it has all the hallmarks that made De la Mare so popular. Its rhythm carries the reader gently but inexorably along, and it is not hard to see why it was set to music.

'Something huge and warm . . . like a living prow': Martin Lanz with his working donkey, see p.116

Nicholas Nye was lean and grey,
Lame of leg and old,
More than a score of donkey's years
He had been since he was foaled;
He munched the thistles, purple and spiked,
Would sometimes stoop and sigh,
And turn to his head, as if he said,
'Poor Nicholas Nye!'

Alone with his shadow he'd drowse in the meadow,
Lazily swinging his tail,
At break of day he used to bray,
Not much too hearty and hale;
But a wonderful gumption was under his skin,
And a clean calm light in his eye,
And once in a while, he'd smile,
Would Nicholas Nye.

Seem to be smiling at me, he would,
From his bush in the corner, of may,
Bony and ownerless, widowed and worn,
Knobble-kneed, lonely and grey;
And over the grass would seem to pass
'Neath the deep dark blue of the sky,
Something much better than words between me
And Nicholas Nye.

But dusk would come in the apple boughs,
The green of the glow-worm shine,
The birds in nest would crouch to rest,
And home I'd trudge to mine;
And there, in the moonlight, dark with dew,
Asking not wherefore nor why,
Would brood like a ghost, and as still as a post,
Old Nicholas Nye.

The best known donkey poem must be G.K. Chesterton's, written at much the same time. Cleverly, Chesterton throws all the insults available at the poor animal, until its triumphant come-back in the final verse – a classic case of the donkey having the last word.

> When fishes flew and forests walked
>   And figs grew upon thorn,
> Some moment when the moon was blood
>   Then surely I was born.
>
> With monstrous head and sickening cry
>   And ears like errant wings,
> The devil's walking parody
>   On all four-footed things.
>
> The tattered outlaw of the earth,
>   Of ancient crooked will;
> Starve, scourge, deride me: I am dumb,
>   I keep my secret still.
>
> Fools! For I also had my hour;
>   One far fierce hour and sweet:
> There was a shout about my ears,
>   And palms before my feet.

The French poet Francis Jammes, who wrote lyrical poems about country life at the turn of the nineteenth century, asked that his journey to Paradise should be in the company of donkeys:

> Let me come with these donkeys, Lord, into your land,
> These beasts who bow their heads so gently and stand
> With their small feet joined together in a fashion
> Utterly gentle, asking your compassion.
> I shall arrive, followed by their thousands of ears,
> Followed by those with baskets at their flanks,
> By those who lug the carts of mountebanks
> Or loads of feather-dusters and kitchen-wares,
> By those with humps of battered water-cans . . .
> In that haven of souls let it be that, leaning above
> Your divine waters, I shall resemble these donkeys,
> Whose humble and sweet poverty will appear
> Clear in the clearness of your eternal love.

D.H. Lawrence's 'The Ass' was written while he was living in Sicily, land of donkeys. His poems about birds, beasts and flowers are a joyous mixture of acute observation and the unexpected – and 'The Ass' is no exception. This is a randy ass, whose bray is a long drawn out shout 'ending on a grunt of agonised relief'.

> Somehow, alas, he fell in love,
> And was sold into slavery.

> He fell into the rut of love,
> Poor ass, like man, always in rut,
> The pair of them alike in that.

> All his soul in his gallant member
> And his head gone heavy with the knowledge of desire
> And humiliation.

Ted Hughes, countryman and consummate nature poet, managed to get inside the skin of many of his animal subjects in a truly inspired fashion. In *What Is the Truth?*, a long narrative poem in which God and his Son visit mankind in order to ask some pertinent questions about life on earth, a farmer's daughter describes to them her donkey:

> But here he is in the nettles, under the chestnut leaves,
> With his surprising legs,
> Such useful ready legs, so light and active.

> And neat round hooves, for putting down just anywhere,
> Ready to start out again this minute scrambling all over Tibet!

> And his quite small body, tough and tight and useful,
> Like travellers' luggage,
> A thing specially made for hard use, with no trimmings,
> Nearly ugly. Made to outlast its owner. . . .

> But mostly he's comical – and that's what I like.
> I like the joke he seems
> Always just about to tell me. And the laugh,
> The rusty, pump-house engine that cranks up laughter
> From some long-ago, far-off, laughterless desert . . .

Who can compete with that? Many have tried, for some truly sad and bad poems have been written about donkeys, as a trawl through the Internet will verify. It is as if the donkey, abused and mocked as it has been, speaks to other lost souls, offers companionship in their pain and loneliness.

The contemporary American poet Robert Bly found comfort in his old age as well as the title for his latest book of poems in talking into the ear of a donkey. ('Even the word "donkey" is a joy to me,' he writes in a letter, 'let alone its ear!')

> I have been talking into the ear of a donkey.
> I have so much to say! And the donkey can't wait
> To feel my breath stirring the immense oats
> Of his ears. 'What has happened to the spring,'
> I cry, 'and our legs that were so joyful
> In the bobblings of April?' 'Oh, never mind
> About all that,' the donkey
> Says. 'Just take hold of my mane, so you
> Can lift your lips closer to my hairy ears.'

'Oh, never mind about all that' might be the perfect epitaph for the donkey.

─── CHAPTER 9 ───

DONKEYS
in art

As in literature, the donkey stereotypes are there in art, high or low, sacred or profane, Old Master or cartoon. In a fifth-century mosaic pavement from Constantinople a donkey languidly spurns the advances of a young man. A painted drinking horn from ancient Greece shows a double-headed animal, half ram, half donkey, both sexual symbols; the donkey's ears are laid back and it is braying. In a drawing by Goya, the young Marquis of Villafranca, suspected of having been killed by his doctors, lies on his deathbed flanked by two donkeys dressed in doctors' gowns.

The Old Testament story of Balaam and the ass has been a favourite subject with many artists, including Rembrandt, but the incident is particularly vividly portrayed in a fourteenth-century Spanish Bible. Here we can feel the anguish of the donkey as Balaam beats it on, his eyes closed to everything except his own needs (see illustration p.18).

The Renaissance fashion for painting scenes from the New Testament gave donkeys a constant part; seldom the star turn, they were almost always present in a supporting role. Literally so in the many depictions of the Flight into Egypt, as the ass humbly carried his precious cargo of Mary and the baby Jesus to safety. Giotto, in a fresco painted in the Scrovegni chapel in Padua during the first decade of the fourteenth century, captures the gait and demeanour of the donkey to perfection. This donkey walks along a narrow ledge in front of a rather unconvincing rock, but most of the European painters of the period

Detail of the flight into Egypt from a Catalan Romanesque altarpiece in Santa Maria de Lluçà, c.1225-50.

ignored the reality of what must have been a taxing journey across harsh terrain, preferring to present the protagonists in the lush landscape of their own homeland. The background in Vittore Carpaccio's *Flight* is positively manicured; the travellers are in their best clothes, and the donkey looks recently groomed. The prize for capturing the essence of donkeyness though must go to the Netherlandish painter Gerard David. In his beautiful and harmonious *Rest on the Flight into Egypt* of 1510, the Virgin, draped in a luminous blue robe, sits alone with her child at centre stage of an idyllic landscape. The small grey donkey to the left is looking on, doing what donkeys love doing best – grazing the bank at head level. An apocryphal story tells how when the family paused to rest they were hungry as well as weary, but were unable to gather dates from the tall palm trees. So Jesus commanded the tree to lower its branches – a miracle that would have been appreciated by the donkey too, no doubt. In David's picture the tree is a chestnut, and Joseph is just bashing the fruit down with a stick. And in a charming study by the sixteenth-century Spanish painter Juan de Borgoña it is the Child himself who is picking fruit, while the unbridled donkey takes the opportunity to snatch a bite too.

The donkey in Caravaggio's more dramatic and sensual painting (1596-97) of the Holy Family at rest during their flight is also half hidden to the left, though here he is very much a part of the group. And he looks to be doing what donkeys are also very prone to do – leaning his weight on a shoulder, here that of Joseph, who is holding the music from which the angel plays his violin.

A wonderfully alert donkey is unusually prominent in a Nativity scene painted on a wooden panel by a thirteenth-century unknown Master of Aviá, and most scenes from the Nativity have included the ox and the ass of the Biblical story. The ass in Melchior Broederlam's *Nativity* *c*.1400, an unconvincing, stuffed, Eeyore-like animal, stands close

The Flight into Egypt, c.1515, Vittore Carpaccio.

enough to be nuzzling the baby's halo. Another painting on wood from an altarpiece panel, *c*.1457, has a very realistic donkey apparently bowing (or sniffing, as donkeys do) at Joseph's back. The egg tempera gives the painting a diffuse luminosity, and the donkey's white underparts positively glow. (This strangely modern representation has a midwife folding a sheet on the left, though the baby Jesus is enormous and Mary immaculate as ever.) In Fra Diamante's *Nativity* the ox and the ass are framed between Mary and Joseph, rather improbably nose-to-nose but once again very much part of the proceedings. What is striking is the different characters these Renaissance donkeys have.

Religious themes, particularly Biblical ones, are not currently fashionable, but Roger Loveless is a contemporary artist who has made them something of a trademark. *In the Hands of the Father* is a modern Nativity scene, with a very hands-on father and a white-nosed donkey standing guard while Mary sleeps.

Jesus choosing to ride into Jerusalem on an ass was a symbolic act, fulfilling the Old Testament prophecy. Isaiah's prediction of the Saviour, 'He was oppressed, and he was afflicted, yet he opened not his mouth', could well be applied to the the animal who bore him to the place of his betrayal and death. It is also perhaps signficant that, in St Mark's version of the story, Jesus instructs two of his disciples to fetch a colt, 'whereon never man sat'. 'And they went their way, and found the colt tied by the door without in a place where two ways met . . . And they brought the colt to Jesus, and cast their garments on him; and he sat upon them.' This untrained colt needed no breaking in, no fancy trappings.

In a very early depiction of this scene, from an eleventh-century German benedictional by an unknown illuminator, the tiny colt is more like a dog than an ass, with emaciated neck and enormous ears even for a donkey. The Flemish Renaissance painter Simon Bening has a more convincing donkey, though the procession is passing through a very European landscape and the 'palms' being picked to throw before their feet come from the nearest equivalent, an ash tree. A nineteenth-century watercolour by James Tissot shows the colt and

The Foal of Bethphage, one of a series of many depictions of the life of Christ painted by James Tissot between 1884 and 1896

its mother being collected by the disciples. (Tissot was an amazingly prolific French artist who produced a series of more than seven hundred watercolour drawings of scenes from the Old and New Testaments, travelling to Palestine in his search for first-hand background material.)

The saints were a popular subject in early religious art, and those associated with donkeys, St Francis and more specifically St Anthony, are well represented. Giovanni Bellini's *St Francis in the Desert* has a donkey standing alone in a green field that mysteriously gives way to a cliff, in a landscape that is hard to associate with the desert but is nonetheless very beautiful. The saint is in an ecstatic state – the picture was originally called 'St Francis in Ecstasy' – barefoot, and wearing the familiar Franciscan habit which was then of a lighter brown. The brown donkey has the dorsal and shoulder stripes of the Crucifixion.

An early stained-glass window from Innsbruck depicts the story of St Anthony and the trial of the Holy Sacrament, see p.69. The donkey kneels, rather uncomfortably since donkeys are not designed to do so, while the saint proffers the monstrance. A similarly uncomfortable but very alert donkey is seen from the rear in Taddeo Crivelli's *St Anthony of Padua*, painted in tempera and gold leaf *c*.1469. At much the same time, Donatello was making *The Miracle of the Ass* as part of a bronze relief celebrating the miracles of St Anthony, in the Basilica di Sant'Antonio in the saint's native town of Padua.

♦ ♦ ♦

Of more modern donkeys in art, Chagall's best known ones are anatomically conventional despite being coloured blue, green or yellow, but in *La Femme à tête d'âne* he gave his imagination free rein. Here a curvaceous dame cavorts by moonlight; she wears a close-fitting jacket and knickerbockers and sports a smiling donkey's head, although with very modest ears. A jewelled ruff conveniently hides the join between woman and beast. A real donkey stands in the background, a red tophat on its head. What are we to make of this? Chagall would reply, 'If a symbol should be discovered in a painting of mine, it was not my intention. It is a result I did not seek. It is something that may be found afterwards, and which can be interpreted according to taste.'

Contemporary tales of people travelling with donkeys as companions are usually illustrated with photographs, but when R.L. Stevenson made his journey in 1879 this was not an option. The first edition, published that year, did not have illustrations, but a new edition published in 1907 contained engravings by Walter Crane, including this much reproduced frontispiece, see p.14. Here we have the author reclining – fully dressed and looking suitably nonchalant – in his 'sleeping-sack' while the poor animal stands rather mournfully beside him, also fully dressed in her pack saddle. At least it has been unloaded. Several other scenes from the travels are depicted in the background, finishing off with an into-the-sunset silhouette at the very top, but that this should be Modestine is hard to believe. Modestine, 'not much bigger than a dog', 'inimitably small', dwarfed by her pack? Crane was a well-respected illustrator, but he hadn't done his homework here.

La Femme à tête d'âne, 1927, Marc Chagall.

Platero has been portrayed by many different artists over the years, who have made him look like everything from hairy old hack to young beauty. There are statues of him too, looking coltish in the author's home town of Moguer, and lumpy in the Parque de Málaga.

There are times when illustrations detract from a book. The English edition of *Culotte the Donkey*, published in 1976 just after its author Henri Bosco had died, was illustrated with line drawings by John Ward. These to my mind add nothing to the vivid word portraits painted by the author, which are best left to the imagination.

One's image of Eeyore is probably defined by whether one grew up with the line drawings of E.H. Shepard or the Walt Disney version. Neither do donkeys in general or Eeyore in particular much of a favour: Shepard makes him look spineless, while Disney has him as a badly stuffed cushion. None of these have been well served by their illustrators; catching the donkey essence, avoiding the cute or the wooden, is not easy.

Depressed by the caricatures and demeaning cartoon figures of the donkey in so much so-called art, I was cheered to come across some going about their business on French civic coats-of-arms: calm and dignified, conscious of their useful role in the affairs of men, in heraldic terms they symbolise the virtues of patience and humility.

Coat-of-arms of Azet, a commune in the Hautes-Pyrénées.

CHAPTER 10

DONKEYS
in other roles

POSTCARDS

Picture postcards became popular in Britain in the late nineteenth century. As the postal service took off, so too did the boom in seaside holidays, both the result of easier, quicker, cheaper transport, particularly by train. Suddenly everyone went on holiday, usually to the seaside – and most people sent postcards home. Cards to Acacia Avenue and Badgerwood Drive, to Mum and Dad and Aunt Elsie, 'Weather could be better' being the usual cry, with the occasional 'Sunny today' and more frequent 'Pouring again'. It was on the beach that the association between donkeys and postcards was first made. Quite why donkey rides almost always took place on the beach is not

No. 236   DONKEYS ON THE SANDS, WESTON-SUPER-MARE

clear, apart from the obvious bonus of soft landings. And perhaps, when sunbathing was not much of an option due to the amount of clothing that had to be worn, and swimming ditto, bored holidaymakers needed a harmless pastime.

Since then donkeys have adorned holiday postcards from Brighton to Benidorm, often sporting silly hats or otherwise being made to look either cute or stupid, sometimes both. But some show them earning their keep in more serious ways, such as the mobile shops of southern Spain, see p.49. A c.1890 card has a diminutive donkey on a Cornwall beach dwarfed by a load of seaweed, which was then highly prized as a fertiliser. An atmospheric shot on the beach in Gibraltar, taken in 1936, shows fishermen loading up donkeys with their catch to be transported to the local market.

Today makers of postcards and greetings cards – surely a flagging industry in the age of e-mails – tend to go for the donkey as joker, with head-on shots of mouthfuls of teeth, yawning or braying, far removed from the image of the dear little donkey. Donkeys too have their vulgar side.

And to get the postcards there, donkeys have made an appearance on postage stamps from Switzerland to Mongolia. A series of farm animals on French postage stamps circulated in 2004 included 'Le Baudet' (*baudet* an alternative for *âne* in French), an attractive long-haired donkey, a Poitou, snuffling the ground in characteristic donkey fashion.

ADVERTISING AND LOGOS

Given the donkey's reputation for stupidity and stubbornness, it may seem an odd choice as a symbol for a political party. Now demoted as its official logo, the donkey remains the emblem of the US Democratic Party. Its adoption is a strange story. The originator is usually given as the well-known cartoonist Thomas Nast, whose cartoon 'A Live Jackass Kicking a Dead Lion', published in 1870, shows a donkey labelled Copperhead Press (the Copperheads were a group of Democrats who strongly opposed the Civil War) lashing out its heels at the Republican Secretary of War, Edwin Stanton, who had just died – a dig at the anti-war beliefs of the Democrats. The Democrat–donkey association began much earlier, however, before Thomas Nast was born. Andrew Jackson,

while running for president in 1828, was labelled by his opponents a
'jackass' – an obvious pun on his name – but cleverly turned it to his
advantage by praising the donkey's willpower and using it on his
campaign posters. This was a gift in waiting for the cartoonists,
though the first political cartoon to use the donkey did not appear until
1837, when 'The Modern Balaam and His Ass' showed the former
president Jackson still trying to direct the donkey, his party, in the
direction he wanted. This brought a flurry of donkey cartoons in the
late 1800s. A reversible drawing, very fashionable at the time,
published in America *c*.1861 portrays Jefferson Davis, then President of
the Confederacy, 'subdued' as an ass's head and, upside down,
'rampant'. A contemporary cartoon by the same artists also features

Davis as an ass, in its pejorative sense – though a very elegant one – confronting the Republican elephant. (The choice of an elephant as the Republican emblem is seemingly just as open to ridicule as the Democratic donkey, though it too was used first as an insult and then defiantly taken up as a symbol of strength and dignity.)

But in a cartoon of *c.*1900 in the *New York Herald* the donkey is shown representing Congress, which had a Republican majority at the time. In a parody of the dilemma faced by Buridan's ass (see p.34), the donkey is seen deliberating between the choice of whether a canal to link the Pacific with the Atlantic should go through Panama or Nicaragua. The Senate didn't make up its mind for another two years.

The donkey as Democratic emblem featured in many cartoons during the 2008 presidential campaign. In one, Hillary Clinton sits astride a stitched together donkey with the caption 'Hillary Clinton whips the unified Democratic donkey'. Another, on the same topic, is captioned 'In a field just outside of Denver' and shows a 'unified' Democratic donkey with its front half, feet on the ground, labelled Obama and the rear end with its legs in the air and a Clinton ticket hanging from its tail.

Unlike some of its striped and bestarred or flag-draped predecessors, the current Democratic donkey is less of a caricature, more a symbol of freedom in the acrobatic flourish of its hindlegs, which echoes that of the original Nast cartoon. And despite its demotion, it has lost none of its popularity. In the run-up to the presidential election of 2012 it can be seen alive and kicking not only on posters and T-shirts but on magnets and mousepads, wall clocks and pillows and, with feet more or less firmly on the ground, as a lawn inflatable. Maybe a donkey in the White House garden, alongside the famous herb patch, would be a shrewd political move.

Democratic logo

This perfect Catalan donkey could have been the model for the famous silhouette.

A donkey took a leading role in the 2012 election campaign in Russia when the leader of the Liberal Democratic Party, Vladimir Zhirinovsky, released a video of himself on a sleigh drawn by a black donkey called Proshka. This was a clumsy attempt to liken the 'little wretched donkey' to the current condition of Russia, which Zhirinovsky pledged to restore to its former glory as a troika, the very fast three-horse sleigh that symbolises Russia. 'When I become president things will get moving again,' he boasted. But the stunt backfired as he then whipped the donkey, which produced a flurry of complaint and merely enhanced Zhirinovsky's reputation as a tasteless joker without political weight.

In Spain the Catalan donkey, a silhouette known to thousands through its use as a car sticker, was adopted as the symbol for the Catalan nationalist cause. This was in deliberate contrast to the famous bull silhouette, originally an advertisement for Osborne brandy and subsequently the most popular car sticker, which presented a very different aspect of Spanish culture. The image of the Catalan donkey, a breed in its own right, became the subject of a copyright lawsuit; the original silhouette was commissioned by the Association for the Promotion of the Catalan Asinina Race, who were not pleased to have it taken over for political ends. The sticker promoters were obliged to modify the design in 2004 by removing the donkey's testicles. No wonder it looks a trifle pathetic.

A donkey that is not at all pathetic is the star of a video ad for Budweiser beer that was voted the best commercial during the 2004 Super Bowl. A small donkey watches a team of Clydesdales pulling a dray and sighs, 'All my life I've wanted to be a Clydesdale.' We see the little donkey practising walking like a Clydesdale, pulling a tiny cart (with a case of Budweiser in the back), even trying 'hair extensions', the enormous characteristic Clydesdale feathers on its legs. Then comes the interview, and the diminutive donkey is led into a stable to confront a row of gigantic carthorses. 'What makes you think you can be a Clydesdale, son?' rumbles one. The answer is the only one a donkey can give: a resounding bray. Next scene, our donkey is harnessed up and leading the team of eight horses. 'I must have said something right,' he says jauntily.

What made this so popular? Apart from the smallness of the donkey and the magnificence of the Clydesdales, it must have something to do with the triumph of the underdog, the David and Goliath syndrome with which we all identify. But it is also acute about the donkey nature: that, unassuming though it is, through determination and hard work it will come through in the end.

FILM

There are several films featuring donkeys, but only one with a donkey as its protagonist. In *Au Hasard Balthazar*, a black and white film made in 1966 by the French director Robert Bresson, Balthazar is present throughout, from the ringing bray that accompanies the opening credits to the donkey's death with which the film abruptly ends. Having been adopted as a tiny and enchanting foal into a poor family by the daughter, Marie, Balthazar is loved, baptised, and tumbled with in the hay. These idyllic scenes are rudely interrupted as Balthazar, the Black Beauty of the donkey world, undergoes a succession of worsening experiences at the hands of his various owners. At one stage he breaks free and returns to Marie, but she too is caught up in a web of brutish intrigue and the two are parted once more. Balthazar represents the 'friend who will share my pleasures and sorrows' for whom Marie searches in vain; each is mocked and abused, scarred by the passing of time, and Balthazar's final moments, laden with contraband and then abandoned by Marie's own persecutors, come as almost a relief. His troubles are over; may he rest in peace.

The film, factual and understated though it is, has many levels of emotion and meaning: it has even been likened to an allegory of the life of Christ. From our perspective, it is interesting not only in its portrayal of the mutual affection between girl and donkey but also in the consistent dignity shown by an animal so abused by human inhumanity. As the film's blurb neatly puts it, the story is 'underpinned by the donkey's wilful and stubborn refusal of victimhood, prior to eventual acceptance of his destiny.'

Robert Bresson's
au hasard
Balthazar

Contemporary with *Balthazar* (dates vary from 1964 to 1968) was a film directed by Alfredo Castellón based on *Platero y Yo*, see p.88. The film was described, a touch half-heartedly, as a brave attempt to translate Jiménéz's lyrical prose-poem into a visual medium, and seems to be noted mostly for the appearance of the actress María Cuadra, who plays the obligatory love interest, Aguedilla, and so ousts Platero from centre stage.

The relationship between Shrek, the ogre in the animated films based on books by William Steig, and Donkey is finely drawn. They become travelling companions, even though the antisocial and paranoid Shrek, who thinks everyone is judging him, wants to be left to live alone in his swamp. Donkey, faithful and unjudgemental as donkeys are, plays a key role in the complicated adventures and machinations surrounding Shrek and his princess, but as in the best fairytales all ends happily.

There's a donkey too in the Walt Disney film *Fantasia*. In the Bacchanalian scene accompanying Beethoven's Pastoral Symphony, Bacchus has a donkey with a golden horn – a donkey unicorn – called Jacchus, not part of the original myth but an invention of Disney's, the name bridging jackass and Bacchus. But far from being a cartoon parody, Jacchus is a creature who represents speed and strength.

MUSIC

Donkeys and music may seem strange bedfellows, but there are several links. The association of donkeys with Schubert started with *Au Hasard Balthazar* and the Piano Sonata No.20 which acts as the film's leitmotiv. It was taken up by Andy Merrifield, who opens his book thinking about Schubert and later cleverly describes the way in which the music chimes with the donkey character and fate. The Andantino which accompanies the broken Balthazar's lonely death has 'a romance and melancholy that's perfect for a donkey . . . Schubert's piano is the sound of tragic braying, of anybody who lies down, alone, in an empty field, after toiling all their lives without reward.'

In *Carnival of the Animals* donkeys have a major part of their own, appearing in three of the fourteen movements. Written by Saint-Saëns as a bit of fun while he was on holiday in 1866 and already a well-known composer, the piece was not performed in full for another fifty years, until after his death; he forbade its publication during his lifetime because he was afraid that it might detract from his reputation. When the *Carnival* was eventually published it became an instant success – and ironically it is now the work most often associated with Saint-Saëns.

The third movement is called 'Hémiones (animaux véloces)', referring to the fleet-footed wild ass *Equus hemionus*, the onager; two pianos both playing scales in octaves portray the galloping asses. In the eighth, dedicated to 'Personnages à longues oreilles', two violins mimic the donkey's bray as they saw from high to low notes. The movement's title, with its *personnages* – translatable as 'characters' but also as 'very important people' – as opposed to the more obvious *animaux*, is thought to have been a dig at music critics. At the end of the final movement the braying of donkey/critic is heard again. (That word bray was originally used only for donkeys and trumpets, but has more recently been applied to humans in the sense of noisy pronouncements with little validity – a neat combination of trumpeting and the stereotypical 'silly ass'.)

There have been two music groups named The Donkeys: the current folk and rock band from San Diego harks back to a 1970s British group. And if you are really keen, you can watch a video about Dominick, the Italian Christmas donkey, set to music and illustrated with – no, not a donkey but a kicking horse.

---------- CHAPTER 11 ----------

DONKEY
companionship

That donkeys like company, whether of their own kind or not, is well recorded. But what I would like to explore is the satisfaction that humans find in companionship with them. Companionship is a mellow state. It is not challenging, never critical, and by definition mutual.

From Persian kings to Spanish queens, from fictional ten-year-old orphans to world-famous octogenarian artists, people have been drawn to the company of donkeys. For Pepino in *The Small Miracle* Violetta was 'more than just the means of his livelihood. She was mother to him, and father, brother, playmate, companion, and comfort. . . . When there was joy in his heart, he shouted songs into her waving ears; when he was lonely and hurt, he could lean his head against her soft, warm flank and cry out his tears.'

Lara, at four years old, would creep off to the field and spend her time in some silent communication with Dulce known only to the two of them. And when one day Dulce mistook a small finger for a carrot, it was only a few tears and half an hour before the two were reunited.

The company of donkeys is sought in high places. It is well recorded that Queen Victoria liked to be driven round her Balmoral estate in a cart drawn by a donkey, the faithful John Brown in attendance. (Though in the film *Mrs Brown*, the Queen, played by Judi Dench, rode a white pony led by Billy Connolly.) Less well known is Queen Victoria's rescue of an ill-nourished donkey which she came across while walking beside the lake at Acquisgrana, Aachen, where she often spent holidays. Disturbed by the donkey's pitiable state, she asked the peasant owner if it was for sale. 'That depends,' replied the canny man. 'How much did you pay for it?' asked the Queen. On hearing the sum she promptly doubled it; the owner went off happily to spend his loot and Jocko, as she named him, was taken off to live the life of Riley. The tale has a little donkey flick to it, however, for when the following year the peasant saw his donkey, fat, well groomed and decked out in fancy harness, he said wistfully, 'Ah, why didn't I sell myself too when I had the chance . . .'

Queen Victoria accompanied by Princess Beatrice leaving Windsor Castle for a drive in her donkey carriage, 1895.

The Spanish Queen Sofía, a descendant of Victoria on both sides of her family, shares her love of donkeys: pictures of her nuzzling and embracing donkeys abound, in newspapers and her many biographies.

Queen Sofía is given a warm greeting at the Adobe donkey sanctuary in Rute, near Córdoba, September 2008.

—Alguien importante le ha debido de dar un beso y se ha vuelto un vanidoso

'Someone Important gave him a kiss and it's gone to his head.'

Queen Sofía's visit to a sanctuary near Córdoba in September 2008 produced not only great photo opportunities but a follow-up cartoon.

Despite his noble birth Anthony Ashley-Cooper, 7th Earl of Shaftesbury, was a tireless worker for the underdog. In the second half of the nineteenth century, factory workers, miners, chimney sweeps and street traders all benefited from his lobbying on their behalf. Much revered and fêted though he was for his work, the earl claimed that the reward that gave him most pleasure was the gift of a donkey from the costermongers of London, which spent its last days grazing on the family estate in Dorset.

Unfazed though they appear to be by such blue-blooded attentions, donkeys are the preferred animal of the lowly of the earth. Perhaps, more precisely, of those who deliberately turn their backs on worldly success. Many of the people encountered in these pages who have sought out the company of donkeys fall into this category: Rumi, whose cause was submission and surrender; Nasreddin Hodja, the holy fool; Henry Moore, who refused a knighthood ('titles change one's name and one's opinion of oneself', he wrote in his letter of refusal); John Berger, who in his late forties decided that he wanted nothing to do with those in positions of power; Andy Merrifield, who walked away from a hard-won and successful career to wander through the Auvergne with a donkey in order to find out what he did want.

Riding roughshod, over situations and people, takes place on horses; pride is the horseman's hallmark. Chaucer categorised his pilgrims into those whose pride is signified by their horses – the Summoner, the Pardoner – and those who choose more modest mounts: the Nun's priest, the Plowman.

Sancho Panza's short brush with worldly power, as governor of the island of Barataria – admittedly engineered as a joke – ends abruptly and appropriately in farce, and a humiliated Sancho staggers off to find Dapple. He gives the donkey the kiss of peace on his forehead and delivers a heartfelt tribute: 'Come here, dear companion and friend of mine, my fellow-partner in my trials and sorrows. When I went along with you and had no other thought but the mending of your harness and the feeding of your little carcase, happy were my hours, my days and my years! But since I left you and climbed the tower of ambition and pride a thousand miseries have pierced my soul.' As he saddles up Dapple and prepares to leave his weighty responsibilities behind, he says with relief, 'Let me return to my old freedom.' Dapple and Sancho Panza are well suited, just as, however clapped out Don Quixote's old mare Rocinante may have been, a horse was the appropriate animal for a knight. So what message would Jesus have been giving out if he had chosen to ride into Jerusalem on a prancing stallion, lording it over the crowd? Jesus on a lean donkey – a colt at that – is a more fitting symbol for one about to be betrayed and put to death.

Gandhi's views on power are well known, and he believed in man doing his own menial work. As part of his struggle for the rights of Indians in South Africa he oversaw the production of a weekly newspaper, *Indian Opinion*, on his settlement near Natal. Perhaps a little surprisingly, he replaced the two donkeys that were originally used for turning the handle of the great press with 'four hefty Zulu girls', but he also took his turn at the handle.

Nelson Mandela, who grew up running wild in the veld of his native Transkei, worked as a herd-boy from the age of five. He knew about donkeys. 'I learned my lesson one day from an unruly donkey. We had been taking turns climbing up and down its back and when my chance came I jumped on and the donkey bolted into a nearby thornbush. It bent its head, trying to unseat me, which it did, but not before the thorns had pricked and scratched my face, embarrassing me in front of my friends. Like the people of the East, Africans have a highly developed sense of dignity, or what the Chinese call "face." I had lost face among my friends. Even though it was a donkey that unseated me, I learned that to humiliate another person is to make him suffer an unnecessarily cruel fate. Even as a boy, I defeated my opponents without dishonoring them.' When more than sixty years later, 27 of them spent in prison, Mandela went back to the township of Soweto, his home as a young man, legend has it that he chose to be driven there in a donkey cart.

Martin Lanz, a Swiss who has opted for a primitive life with his family as 'new peasants' in Italy, uses horses and donkeys for transport and ploughing and finds it a 'deeply satisfying experience. Instead of sitting on a tractor for hours or using a power tool with all the noise and vibrations and fumes it produces, I work in the quiet, alongside a friendly, intelligent animal. At the end of the day, instead of feeling worn out, I feel tired but relaxed.'

♦ ♦ ♦

What makes people seek out the company of donkeys? Maybe it is the timelessness, their 'old wisdom'. When the sculptor Henry Moore (who unfortunately did not include any donkeys among his many animal studies) was in his late eighties and no longer able even to draw, he demanded to be driven each day to visit a donkey that belonged to a neighbouring pub. 'He really loved that old donkey. Its name was Brandy, but we renamed it Charlie at his suggestion,' recalled the driver. John Berger, approaching eighty, in the midst of pondering his position as a Marxist, pauses to walk a kilometre down the road, climb over the fence and sit among a group of donkeys. In typically few words he captures the behaviour and attitude of the two mares and two foals, concentrating particularly on their legs, 'all sixteen of them. Their slenderness, their sheerness, their containment of concentration, their surety. . . . Theirs are legs for crossing mountains no horse could tackle, legs for carrying loads which are unimaginable if one considers only the knees, the shanks, the fetlocks, the hocks, the cannon-bones, the pastern-joints, the hooves!' Oddly arranged legs, these, but it is not in order to observe their anatomy that he goes, rather for 'the midday company we offer one another, [in which] there is a substratum of what I can only describe as gratitude.'

Henry Moore talks to Charlie in 1985, the year before he died.

In our current, and admirable, desire to understand animals better, the pitfall of anthropomorphism is ever present. And an awful lot of rot has been written about donkeys. 'In their hearts is the most pure and idealistic region on Earth.' 'Donkeys experience huge anticipation, which can be about worry or gladness.' Etcetera. To which, if I may reply in the same vein, my donkey would doubtless give a derisive harrumph, flick one ear and say, 'Oh yeah? Pull the other one . . .'

But having a special relationship with a donkey is not a modern phenomenon, as Rumi makes clear in his poem about the itinerant Sufi, written in the thirteenth century (p.87). Eight hundred years on, people are still finding pleasure working, travelling and communing with donkeys. In our mechanised age, donkeys put us back in touch with nature, with natural rhythms and cycles, with different and timeless values. This is partly a practical consideration. When you are with a donkey you are likely to be away from the city, from traffic, from the impetus of modern life. You may hear the distant rumble of a motorway, or a jet passing overhead, but they do not impinge. Of course this is equally true of being among many other animals, but there seems to be something particular about being in the company of donkeys.

Some of it is physical. Their size makes them less threatening than horses. Their 'cuteness' – those ears, that topknot, the deep, liquid eyes – their patient stance, their innocence, their air of vulnerability all draw people in. (Even thugs and sadists, probably because of those very qualities.) But the physical attraction is only part of the story.

There is something in the donkey character that puts people in touch not only with Nature – capital N – but with their own deeper nature. It is important, I think, not to fall into the trap of ascribing to the animals themselves a deeper nature. But what donkeys share with the oppressed and ill-used, human and animal, down the ages, is an enclosed quality born of the need to withdraw from contact with a cruel world into a dignified inner space.

Such things are hard to describe, impossible to share with the uninitiated or the sceptical, and should not be analysed too deeply.

The phenomenon is best left unexamined. But because it cannot be proved, do not doubt its existence.

And so the donkey teaches us. Wandering and browsing, stopping and looking, letting go of human timescales, we come to realisations: about the animal itself, about ourselves, about nature and life. Our observations may be corroborated – or not – by those of other people, but they emanate from somewhere, a very primitive somewhere, inside us. There is a magic in this silent communication between man and donkey that has affected people down the ages, and that seems to be fuelled by the unique *inscrutability* of this small animal that is so much more than the sum of its parts. We may try, blindfold, to pin the tail on the donkey – but we will never, with all faculties in full force, quite be able to nail its unique character.

Notes and Sources

p.8
Bein Wine, Stellenbosch,
South Africa.

Andy Merrifield, *The Wisdom of Donkeys*,
Walker Publishing Co., New York,
2008; Short Books,
London, 2009.

p.9
Other Men's Flowers is the title of an
anthology of verse selected by A.P.
Wavell, first published in 1945. The
quote is from Montaigne: 'I have
gathered a posie of other men's flowers
and nothing but the thread that binds
them is my own.'

p.12
Bartholomeus Anglicus was born at
some time before 1203, probably in
England, but he lived first in Paris and
then in Poland until his death in 1272.
He is best known for *De proprietatibus
rerum*, On the Nature of Things, an
early encyclopedia from which this
quotation comes.

Comments on Neddie by Sue Paling,
Sathya Sai Sanctuary, Castlebaldwin,
Co. Sligo, Ireland.

p.13
Robert Louis Stevenson, *Travels with a
Donkey in the Cévennes*, first published
by Everyman, 1925.

p.17
The 'sadness glowing . . .' are the
words of Laurens van der Post, who
attributes this deep sadness, which he
sees in the eyes of all domesticated
animals, to their loss of the
wilderness; he talks of horses 'haunted
by dreams of their birthright of
freedom exchanged for a mess of oats
and straw and the security of
luxurious stables.' *A Far-Off Place*,
Chatto and Windus, 1974.

Henri Bosco, *Culotte the Donkey*,
translated by Sister Mary Theresa
McCarthy, Oxford University Press,
1978.

p.18
Spanish bible: *Biblia Romanceada
Escurialense*, MS I-j-3.

p.22
Suniti Namjoshi, *The Blue Donkey
Fables*, The Women's Press, 1988.

Rumi, *Selected Poems* translated by
Coleman Barks, Penguin Books, 1999.

p.23
John Berger, *Hold Everything Dear*,
Verso, 2007.

p. 28, 35
Elisabeth Svendsen, *Down among the
Donkeys*, Pan Books, 1981.

p.37
Fiona Marshall, 'Domestication of the Donkey', *Proceedings of the National Academy of Sciences* online, 10 March 2008.

p.39
Susan Orlean, *Smithsonian Magazine*, September 2009.

p.40
Dr Alex T. Magaisa, newzimbabwe.com.

pp.41-2
Tim and Jackie Ferrier, Canine Country Club, Morton Folly, Youlstone, Bude.

p.42
The Devon Donkey Sanctuary, Slade House Farm, Sidmouth, Devon.

p.43
Guardian, April 2008.

Hacienda de Los Milagros, Chino Valley, Arizona.

p.44
The American Fondouk, Fez, Morocco.

Orlean, see note on p.39 above.

p.45
The Brooke, 30 Farringdon Street, London EC4A 4HH.

p.52
Graham Robb, *The Discovery of France*, Picador, 2008 (quoted from Olwen H. Hufton, *The Poor of Eighteenth-Century France*, Oxford, 1974).

Public shaming, document dated 23 May 1550, from Rothenburg ob der Tauber, Bavaria.

p.55
Anne Michaels, *Fugitive Pieces*, Bloomsbury, 1997.

p.64
Unpublished Legends of Virgil, Elliot Stock, 1899.

Augusto Monterroso, *The Black Sheep and Other Fables*, 1969.

Legendary Fables of Yriarte translated by George H. Devereux, Boston, 1855.

p.71
Blue Donkey Fables, see note on p.22 above. Cover painting by Beth Higgins.

p.72
Printed in the *Guardian*, December 2008.

p.78
Cervantes, *Don Quixote*, Hachette, Paris, Cassell, London, 1863.

p.79
T.C.Boyle, *Water Music*, Granta, 1998.

Michael Ondaatje, *In the Skin of a Lion*, Martin Secker and Warburg, 1987.

p.80
Paul Gallico, *The Small Miracle*, Michael Joseph, 1951.

p.81
Bronson Potter, *Isfendiar and the Wild Donkeys*, Atheneum, New York, 1967.

p.82
Culotte the Donkey, see note on p.17 above.

p.83
Francis B. Thornton, *The Donkey Who Always Complained*, The World's Work, 1957.

Christopher Rush, *To Travel Hopefully*, Profile Books, 2005.

p.84
Tim Moore, *Spanish Steps*, Jonathan Cape, 2004; Vintage, 2005.

p.85
The Wisdom of Donkeys, see note on p.8 above.

p.87
Rumi, see note on p.22 above.

p.88
Samuel Taylor Coleridge, 'To a Young Jack Ass', written in 1794 when the word donkey was not yet in common use. Coleridge declared in a letter of the same year, 'Owls I respect & Jack Asses I love.'

Platero y Yo, first published 1914; English-Spanish edition edited and translated by Stanley Appelbaum, Dover Publications, 2004.

p.92
Francis Jammes, 'Prière pour aller au Paradis aves les ânes', *Quatorze prières*, 1898; translated by Richard Wilbur, *Collected Poems 1943-2004*, Harcourt Inc., 2004. Another poem attributed to Jammes has these lines, even more relevant now than when they were written: 'Lord, we are on the point of disappearing . . . In Italy we are no more than a hundred thousand. It is true that we are only donkeys, but Homer wrote about us in his sublime verse. You yourself rode one of us. Look after us!'

p.93
D.H. Lawrence, 'The Ass', from *Birds, Beasts and Flowers*, 1923.

Ted Hughes, *What Is the Truth? Collected Animal Poems* vol.2, Faber and Faber, 1984.

p.94
Robert Bly, *Talking into the Ear of a Donkey*, W.W. Norton and Company, 2011.

p.102
Nast cartoon first published in *Harper's Weekly*, 15 January 1870.

p.111
St Pelagia of Antioch (known as either The Harlot or The Penitent) plays the cithara, a lyre-like instrument that has been traced back to 1700 BC, while the man leading the donkey holds a remarkably modern-looking guitar.

p.115
Cervantes, *The Adventures of Don Quixote* translated by J.M. Cohen, Penguin Books, 1950.

Gandhi: Millie Polak, BBC archive interview broadcast May 2004.

p.116
Nelson Mandela, *Long Walk to Freedom*, Little Brown, 1995.

Berger, *Hold Everything Dear*, see note on p.23 above.

Index of Names

Picture Credits